Indianapolis Murals
OUTSIDE PUBLIC ART

Volume II - Cultural Districts and Trails

SylvanArts Press
Indianapolis, IN

This book is dedicated to the muralists with appreciation to my friend Carmen Varela, my brother Jim Flack, my husband John Noble, And Gautam Rao, Professor of Art at Butler University for their help and encouragement.

Library of Congress Cataloging Data

Andrews, Sylvia 1946-
        Indianapolis Murals - Outside Public Art; Volume II
            Cultural Districts and Trails
      61 pp. cm. 20.3 x 25.4
      Includes Bibliographical References
       ISBN   9781438206028

      Also:
   Indianapolis Murals - Outside Public Art; Murals with a Message V. I

   Indianapolis Murals – Graffiti and Street Art, Styles and Artists and More Murals V. III

Front piece - The Nature of Indy - Skyline Mural, Monon Trail between 52nd and 54th Streets, Monon Trail, Chapter 6

CONTENTS

Chapters

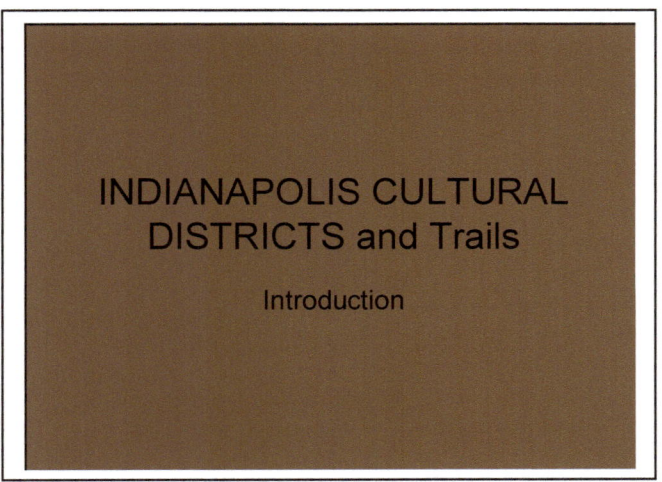

INDIANAPOLIS CULTURAL DISTRICTS and Trails

Introduction

Public Art objects including statues, sculpture and murals are usually appreciated for their artistic value. But art has an economic development component as well. As reporter, S. L. Berry noted in the Indianapolis Star, public art is becoming more prominent in Indianapolis. Indianapolis has an ambitious ten million-dollar cultural tourism initiative under way. A Cultural Development Commission is funding new arts projects, helping clear red tape for permits to place art where it can readily be seen, and putting artists in touch with prospective patrons. While it is at it, the city ought to refurbish some of the urban wall murals it commissioned decades ago. Major public works are part of what will make the city more vibrant. So are smaller, individual contributions. This side of unsupervised graffiti, more individuals and businesses need to become involved in the city's burgeoning art scene. As Mindy Taylor Ross, the city's arts project coordinator, suggested in Berry's article, Indianapolis may lack mountains or an ocean, but its imagination is the only limitation on the works of art that enliven it. [1]

Fig. 2 - Monon Trail, Fall Creek Parkway Trail, Canal Trail and bicycle parking at an event.

TRAILS

Indianapolis has always been fortunate to have many visionary leaders whose ideas and energy have made it a better place. Ray Irvin, director of the Indianapolis Greenways is one citizen whose vision is reshaping our community. Generations from now, people will look back and point with pride at Ray's legacy: miles and miles of trails weaving their way throughout our city, weaving our city back together. [2]

For years, Indianapolis has been assembling the spokes of a marvelous trail system. Now, thanks to the generosity of local donors, this network will have a hub: the Indianapolis Cultural Trail. The 7.5-mile trail will tie together developing cultural districts – the Canal Walk, White River State Park, Fountain Square, Massachusetts Avenue, Indiana Avenue, and the Wholesale District–with pedestrian and bicycle friendly downtown pathways. It also will provide links to the Monon, White River, Eagle Creek, Pogue's Run and Pennsy trails, connecting a network that links distant places throughout the community. Ultimately, it will be the heart of a statewide network of recreational trails. What could be more fitting for a city known as the Crossroads of America for its rail and highway network than creation of a world-class pedestrian and bicycle hub in the heart of Downtown. [2a]

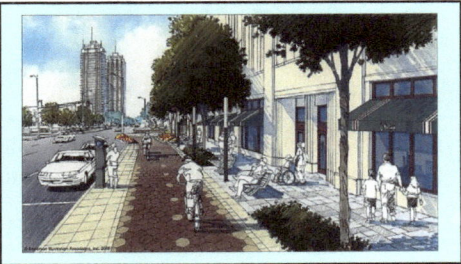

Fig. 2.5 (Artist rendering) Look ahead: Alabama Street looking north to Massachusetts Avenue, as it might look as part of the Indianapolis Cultural Trail. Rundell Ernstberger Associates, LLC

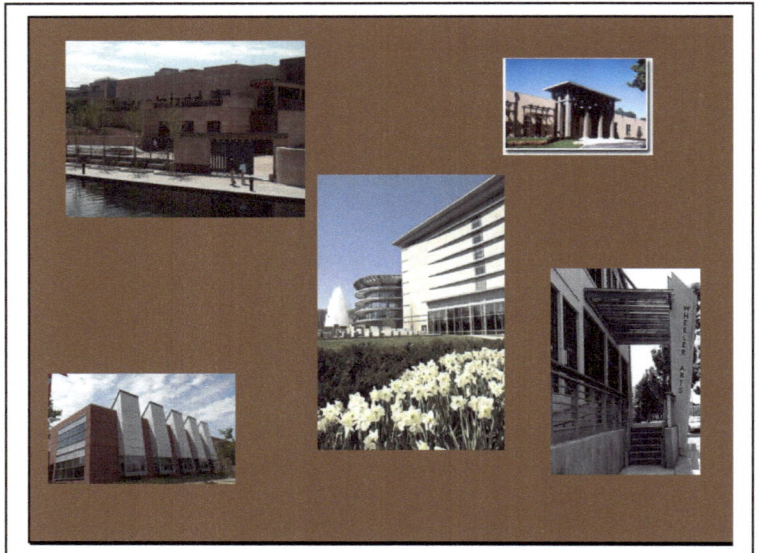

Fig. 3 - Clockwise from top left: Eiteljorg Museum (Canal District), Indianapolis Art Center (Broad Ripple District), Wheeler Art Center (Fountain Square), Indianapolis Museum of Art (38th and Michigan Road – historic Lilly estate), Herron School of Art (near White River and Canal District)

ART INSTITUTIONS in INDIANAPOLIS

The Indianapolis Cultural Development Commission, established in 2002, supports and encourages an environment where the arts and culture flourish. Its nine members and three advisors work together with the Arts Council of Indianapolis, Indianapolis Convention and Visitors Association and Indianapolis Downtown, Inc. (IDI). [3]

OTHER CITIES

Other cities are also participating in Art Education programs to target underprivileged youth at neighborhood sites. They work with the neighbor-hoods to create murals that reflect the culture of the neighborhood. Philadelphia is nationally and internationally recognized as America's "City of Murals." Tucson, Chicago, Los Angeles, San Francisco, Austin Texas and smaller cities such as Lompoc, CA and many other small towns around Indiana and the country are known for their murals.

MCLA in California attempts to preserve some of the older murals in Los Angeles. View their site at: http://www.lamurals.org/Newsletters/0597Newsltr/0597A.html#anchor28505

Fig. 4 - The Cultural Districts Program

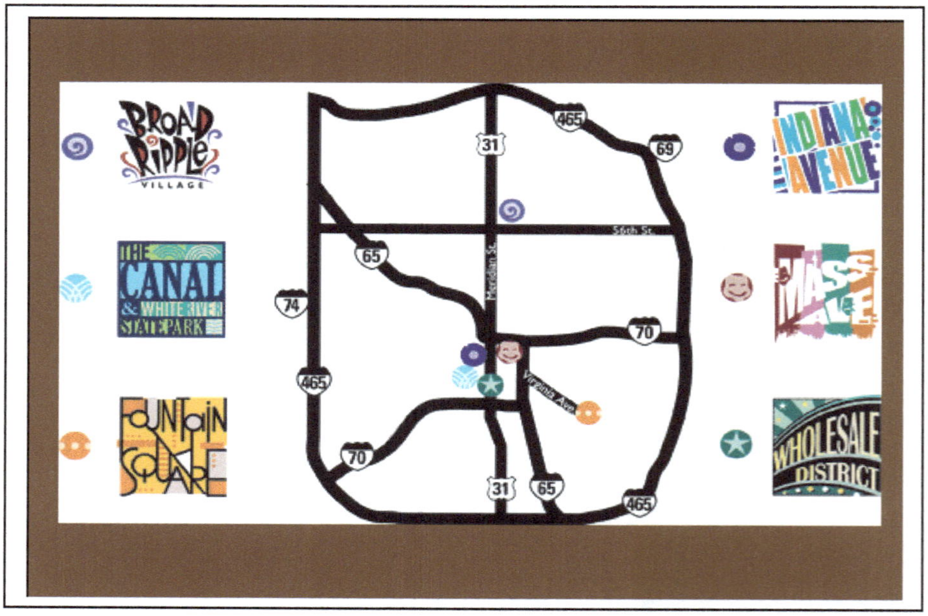

Distinct pockets of cultural opportunity already are thriving in neighborhoods throughout the city. To fully leverage these existing assets, the Cultural Districts Program was created in 2003 to support development efforts in five pilot areas: Broad Ripple Village, Fountain Square, The Canal and White River State Park, Mass Ave Arts & Theater District and the Downtown Wholesale District. In 2004, the Indianapolis Cultural Development Commission approved a sixth district proposal for Indiana Avenue. The following chapters include murals and some history for the six districts.

The Cultural Districts program, one program of the Cultural Tourism initiative, is managed by Indianapolis Downtown, Inc. (IDI) with The Corsaro Group, Ball State University College of Architecture and Planning Indianapolis Center (BSU CAP: IC), and the Cultural Districts Council. [4]

Each cultural district has its own map and list of other attractions that can be found at
.http://www.discoverculturaldistricts.com

Introduction to Indianapolis Cultural Districts - List of photos and sources.

1. Introduction
   [1]Indianapolis Star, Making the city a work of art, June 26, 2004. Editorial Page A14 (star's own editorial)

2. Trails (Fig. 2) and Artist's rendering of proposed cultural trail (Fig. 2.5).
   [2] Ray Irwin: A Man on a Mission, What You May have Missed on the Monon (Michael J. Nolan) mnolan@indianapoliseye.com (online magazine)
   [2a] Indianapolis Star, Cultural path leads to transformation, Oct 14, 2006
   Editorial A12, Indianapolis- Marion County
   [2b] IndyStar.com Metro and State, Oct. 13, 2006; $15M gift paves way for trail by Diana Penner

3. Other Art Institutions
   [3] (Images from the Internet)

4. Indianapolis Cultural Districts map
   [4] http://www.bsu.edu/web/capic/culturalindy/districts.html

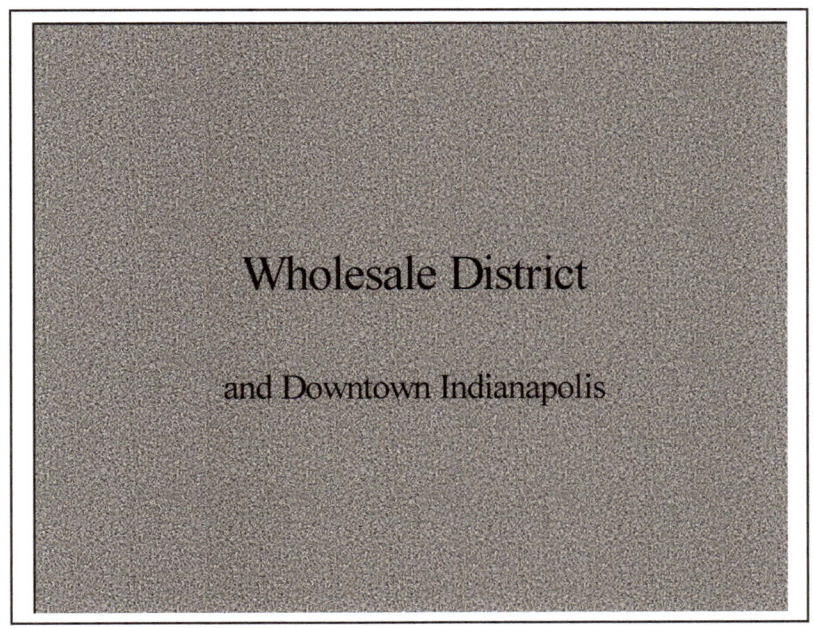

Wholesale District

and Downtown Indianapolis

The Indianapolis Convention and Business Center has this to say about downtown: *Bright lights and marquees highlight the best performances in town. Doormen in tuxedos greet guests. Circle Centre mall delights the most meticulous shoppers. Bustling sidewalks overflow with excited visitors taking in the scenery. Monument Circle welcomes all.*

You're in the Wholesale District in Downtown Indianapolis. For a night (or day) out on the town, you've come to the right place! Amidst Downtown's historic buildings and newest skyscrapers in the heart of the business district, you'll find the biggest names and the brightest attractions the city has to offer. [1] This chapter discusses murals in the wholesale district and some murals that are outside of the wholesale district but still in the downtown area such as the Wyland mural.

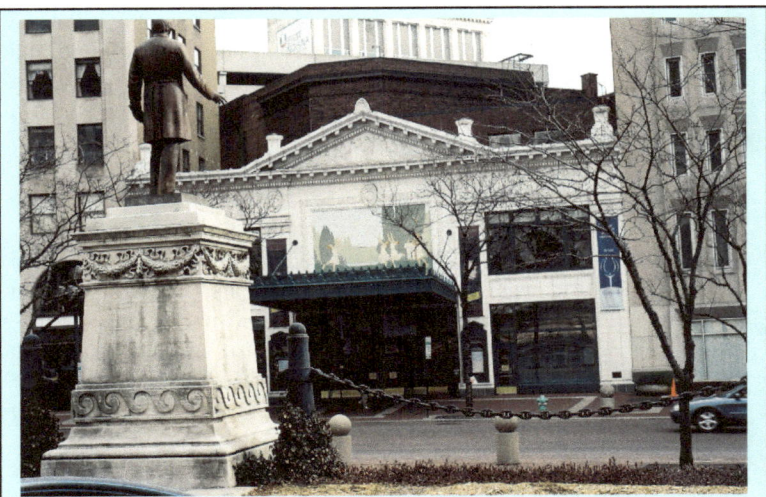

Fig. 1-2 **Circle Theater/Mural** painted by Clifton Wheeler; Circle Theater, 45 Monument Circle, Indianapolis, IN 46204

Unlike many of the larger scale theaters around the state, the Circle Theater was designed in the Neo-Classical style instead of the Spanish Revival Style. Built in 1916, the Circle Theater was one of the first in the Midwest made specifically for feature-length movies. Located on Monument Circle in downtown Indianapolis, it fills a portion of the southeast quadrant of the Circle. Architects Preston Rubush and Edgar Hunter designed the main façade to follow the curves of the road therefore the façade is concave. Covered in white terra cotta, there are a series of subtle exterior decorative features--simple molded panels, a bracketed cornice and pediment across the top, rosettes and swag garlands. However the marquee and a restored Grecian mural dominate the façade. The relatively subdued decorative scheme carries over to the interior. Shades of rose, ivory, and gray prevail throughout. There are plaster moldings and Greek figurines but the senses are not overwhelmed like they would be in a later theater. [2]

The Circle Theater continued to host movies, concerts, and live acts until 1981 although it suffered due to increased competition from suburban multiplexes. It was facing demolition when a series of Indianapolis organizations banded together to save it. In 1982, the Circle underwent a major restoration and celebrated its re-opening in 1984 as the home of the Indianapolis Symphony Orchestra. Indianapolis Power and Light owned the property but they leased it to the Symphony. In 1990 the Symphony was able to purchase the theater and they retain ownership today. [2a]

Fig. 1-3 **The Runners**
Jim McQuiston 1975-76, Acrylic Paint Whole side of the building at 7 East Washington St.

McQuiston, a local architect, won a competition sponsored by the Greater Indianapolis Progress Committee; the idea was to decorate a wall exposed after an adjoining building was destroyed by fire. The mural features several runners in a kind of 1970's pop art style (or cartoon style) and is a whimsical study of color and motion," according to the small plaque at the base.
There was controversy some years ago because some people preferred the Wyland mural that ended up on the IPS building for this wall. [3]

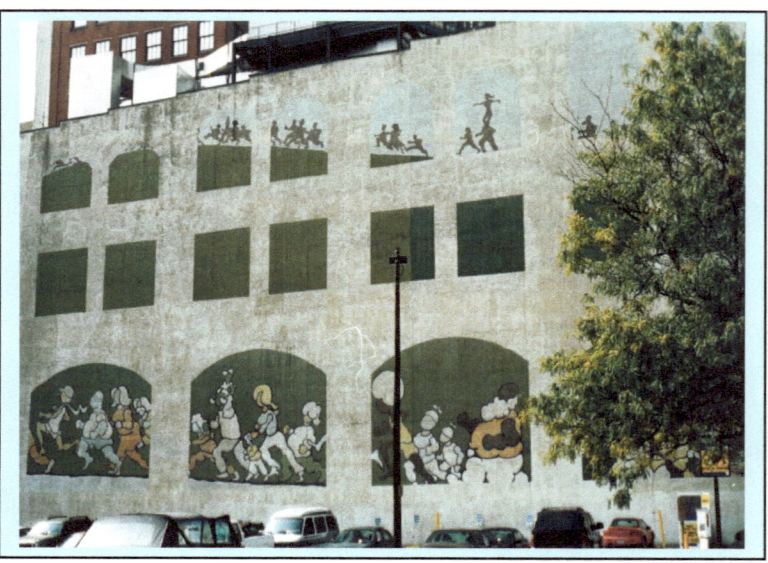

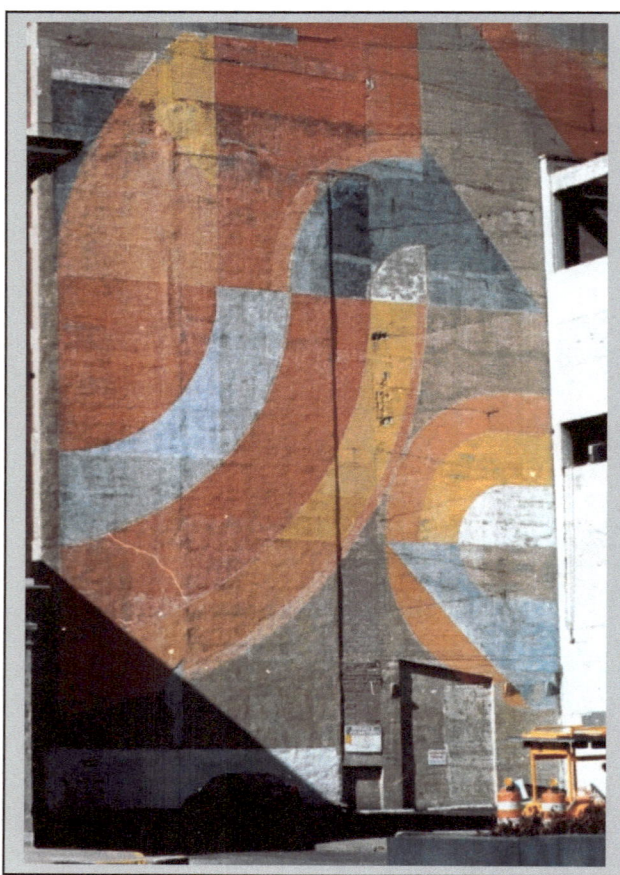

Fig. 1-4 **Urban Wall** - Downtown on Delaware West of City County Building , Roland Hobart

The city of Indianapolis dedicated its first official Urban Wall in 1975. Roland Hobart was the artist and applied the mural to the adjacent walls of the Union Title Building and the Indiana Parking Co. garage at Delaware and Court Streets. Participating in the ceremony were Mayor Richard G. Lugar, Frank McKinney Jr., chairman of the board and president of American Fletcher National Bank, and Dr. Robert Rohn, professor of medicine at Indiana University School of Medicine, who was chairman of the Urban Walls task force. The Indianapolis Department of Parks and Recreation was the sponsor, although its only contribution was the time and administrative abilities of project co-directors Ralph Ogden of the Mayor's Commission on Youth and JoAnne Smithmeyer, of the Parks Department. The National Endowment for the Arts and AFNB paid $3,500 each for the design and completion of the first in what was expected to be a multiyear project involving many other downtown buildings. Hobart's design, a complex puzzle of rectangles, pie-shaped wedges, quarter arcs, and S curves in bold but earthy colors, won out over four other final designs. Hobart is a native of Austria and lived in Shelbyville at the time he painted the mural. He was probably best known for his series of a five-print set commemorating the Indianapolis sesquicentennial and the International Conference on Cities. He now lives in Bloomington and is the National Technical Director for DynaMesh Company in Chicago. He specializes in 3D visualization of Screen Printing. [4]

Fig. 1-5 **International Welcome Walls**
S. Pennsylvania St. Near Conseco Field House
Carol Tharp-Perrin 1999

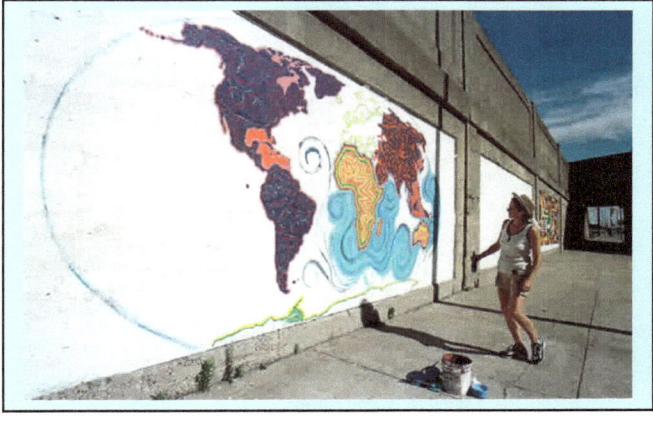

Murals in downtown Indianapolis represent a variety of styles and purposes. Older murals painted mainly for artistic enhancement of the downtown area exist side by side with newer murals painted for a specific occasion such as a mall opening or sports facility opening. Carol Tharp-Perrin, whose murals also can be found on the Martin Luther King Center (North and South Side Chapter and Labor, Race etc. Chapter in
V. 1) and in other Indy locations, other states and even other countries. She has now branched out into other areas of endeavor including performance art and involvement in yoga. A quote from her website follows:

"Over the past 25 years, I have produced hundreds of individual and public participatory paintings, murals and multi-media productions with combinations of private and public funds. These have been provided through universities, corporations, museums, city, state and federal governments, school corporations, neighborhood and merchant associations, a variety of arts organizations and other groups, including the National Endowment for the Arts, the US Department of Education and the US Information Service - Arts America International Visiting Artist Program. Through these years, I have completed a host of artist residencies at museums, schools, hospitals, city parks and communities in North, Central and South America." [5]

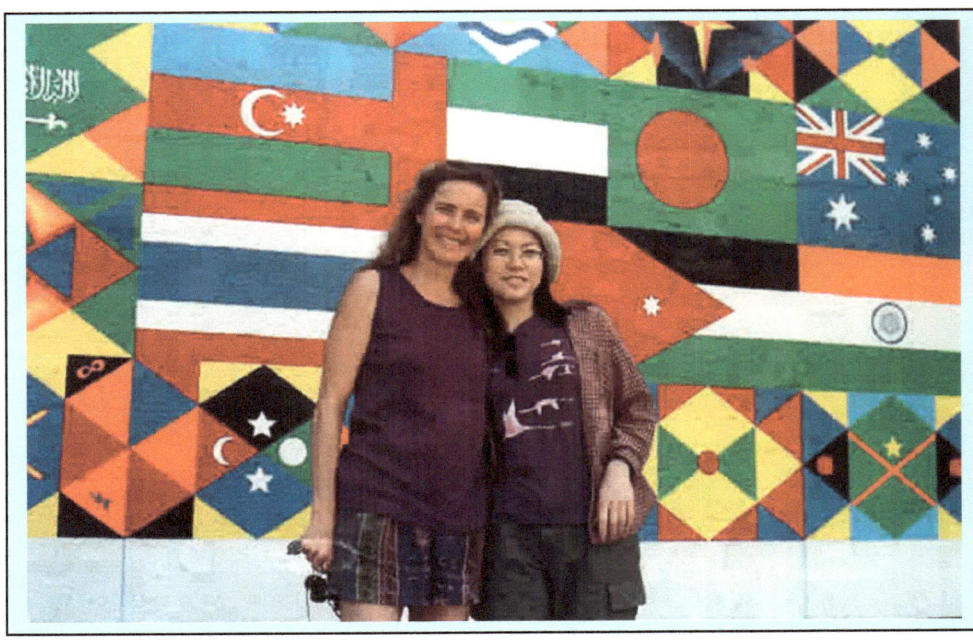

Fig. 1-6 **Carol and Tomoyo painting International Welcome Walls near Conseco.**
The International Welcome Walls located on South Pennsylvania Avenue, just south of the Conseco Fieldhouse in downtown Indian-apolis.
Carol Tharp-Perrin 1999
The first Urban Walls were painted in 1976. In 1999 the new international ones were painted and some of the old ones on Pennsylvania and Georgia were repainted.
The ones on Pennsylvania and Delaware were the first ones in the history of the city (commissioned by the city) and she painted them with Roland Hobart who also painted the mural on Delaware across from the City-County building on page 6. When they built Conseco, they asked her to reconfigure some of the designs on Delaware, and she also did new designs for the International Walls. Students from Franklin College and middle schools and high schools helped by creating quilting pieces that would fit together and Carol pulled them all together. [6]

Fig. 1-7 and 1-8 Same as previous

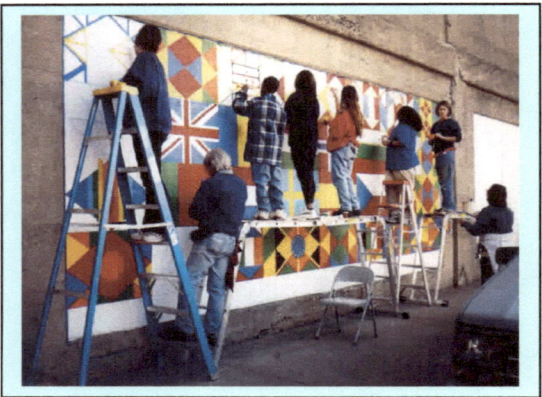 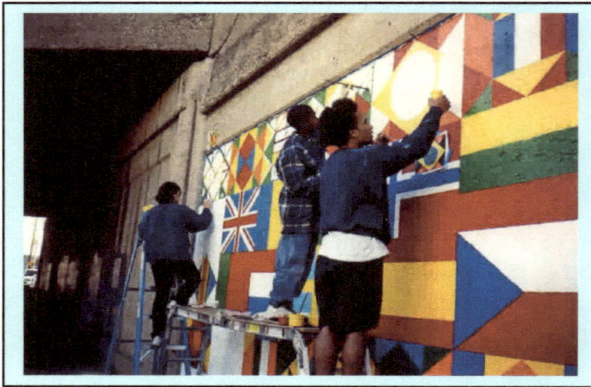

Fig. 1-9 Same as previous

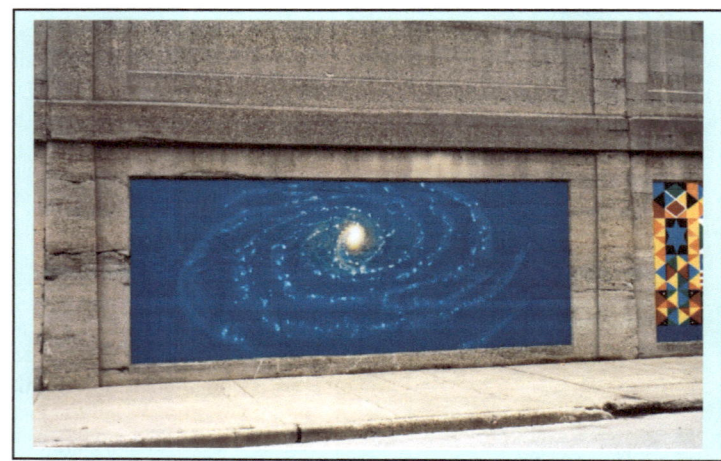

Fig. 1-10 **Urban walls** on Delaware first painted in 1976 and repainted in 1999 by Carol Tharp-Perrin and students.
These mural panels are located directly across from Conseco Field House on Delaware Street, in downtown Indianapolis.

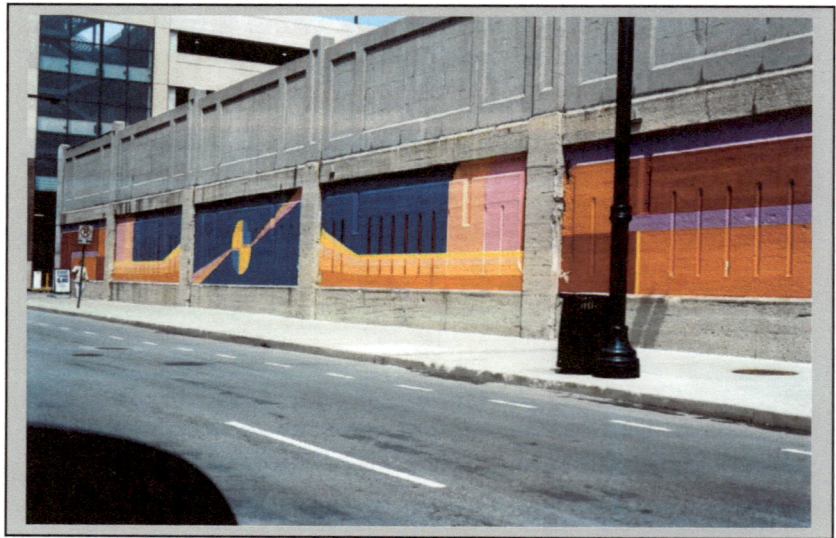

Fig. 1-11 **Circle Center Mall Roof**
Carol Tharp-Perrin, Larry Ginhardt and
Herron Students 1999

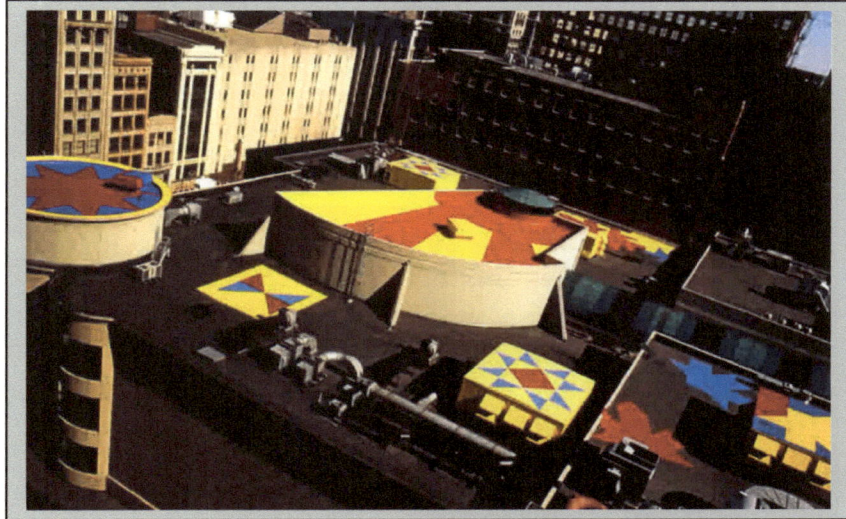

"I probably look down there a lot more than I used to. Visually it's just pleasing and different, very unexpected," said June Davison (National City Center). Like Davison, thousands of Indianapolis office workers can now view the completed mural from the middle and upper floors of surrounding skyscrapers such as One Indiana Square, and American United Life. What's more, the mural is also in the flight pattern of the Indianapolis International Airport, allowing airline passengers daily glimpses of this giant quilt in the sky. The mall mural is also one of the few in the world to span the top of a building, said Carol Tharp-Perrin, coordinator of the Herron School of Art project. Together with her husband, photographer Larry Ginhart, Tharp-Perrin led dozens of Herron students in their daunting three-year quest to complete the project.

With the Indianapolis skyline as their backdrop, the students battled rain, wind, snow and sizzling temperatures to turn this dismal landscape into a kaleidoscope of color. They called it their "gallery in the sky" - a rooftop canvas that covers 186,000 square feet of the largest, lowest building in Downtown Indianapolis. According to their figures, this makes it the world's largest mural. [11] (Not confirmed)

Fig. 1-12 **Circle Center Mall Roof**
Fig. 1-12.5 **Students working**

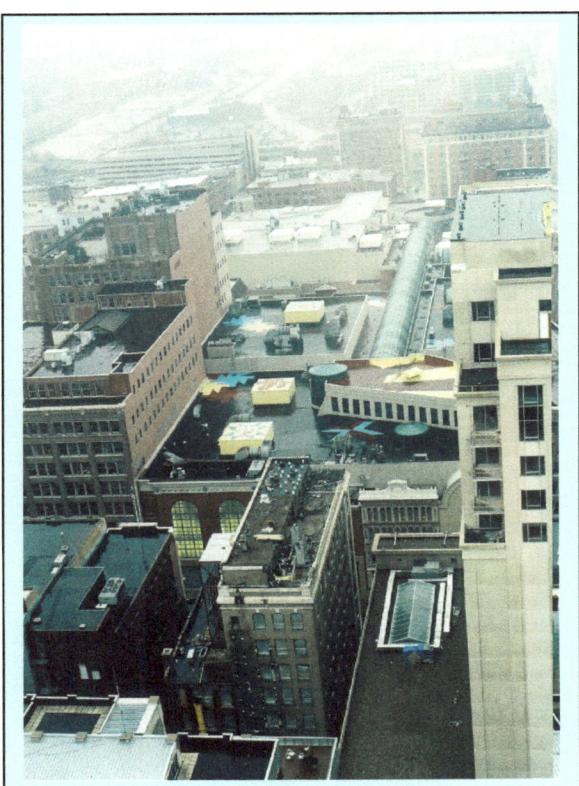

Working from architectural blueprints, the students had to calculate every line, angle and curve of the mural mathematically. They even painted the large air-handling units that dot the rooftop, giving the mural a three dimensional effect.

"I think it's for the spirit of the city, especially for people who work in those buildings," added Angelica Vergara, a former Herron art student. "Beauty is for your soul."

But creating it can be hard work: hand-scrubbing the entire surface, lugging gallons of paint and hoses up several flights of stairs, enduring driving winds and sizzling rooftop temperatures that often reached 100 degrees in summer. Over time, occasional re-application of paint and a protective acrylic sealant will be needed to preserve the life of the mural.[12]

Roughly the size of five and a half football fields, the vibrant design of interlocking quilt patterns depicts falling leaves, circles,

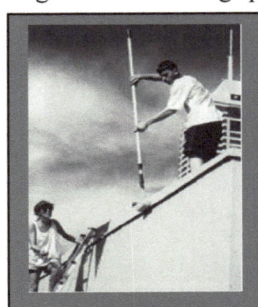

fans, squares and stars in bright, primary colors. It was created by former Herron student N. Beth Line, whose winning entry, "Captivating Quilts", was chosen four years ago (from 1999) in a Herron competition. The simple beauty of familiar quilt patterns, such as the Indiana Reel and the Indiana Star inspired her. But the quilting theme is also symbolic of the collaborative nature of the project.

"We got down on our hands and knees and just did it," said Rita Fox, a former Herron student and IPS elementary art teacher who helped paint the mural. "Just knowing that it will be enjoyed by thousands of people for years to come was worth every bruise and aching muscle." [12a]

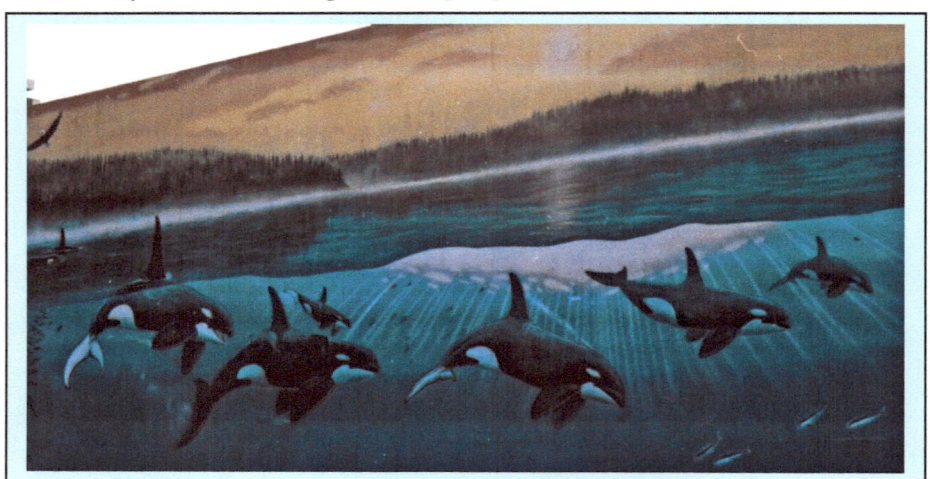

Fig 1-13 **Indianapolis Public Schools Building Mural** - 120 E. Walnut St., Indianapolis, IN Wyland 1997
Wyland bills himself as the world's Premier Ocean Artist and has been painting since 1971. He has completed more than 84 of his Whaling walls throughout the world and has galleries around the country. He has raised the planet's environmental consciousness as far as the ocean and its inhabitants.

Since its inception in 1993 the Foundation's mission has been to inspire people of all ages to protect and preserve the ocean through art and education. In 1998, Wyland supported the United Nations' mission of raising global awareness about our oceans by launching the Wyland Ocean Challenge. Endorsed by the UN and former Vice President Al Gore, Wyland and his team of environmental supporters toured all 50 states in America in 50 days, teaching students through art, science, and hands-on exhibits. At the conclusion of the tour, the program had reached 1 million students. Touring began again in 2003 and will continue through 2008. [13]

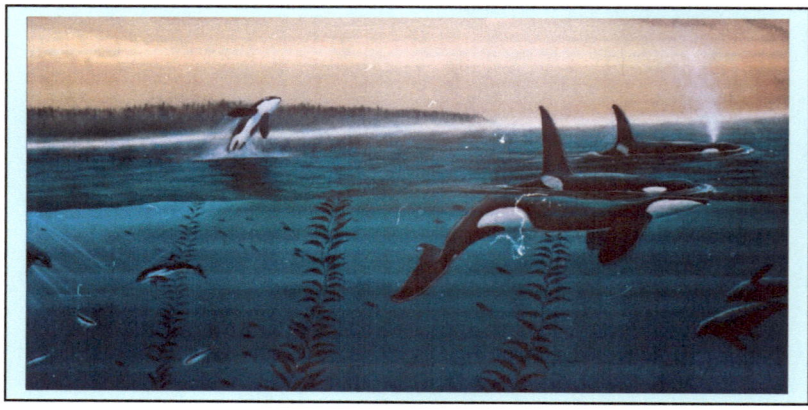

Fig. 1-14 **Orca's Passage**
The Indianapolis Public Schools building was a perfect location for Wyland's 74th Whaling Wall being the location of the Indianapolis Superintendent of Schools. Wyland was supplied with his favorite audience his entire week in Indianapolis, children. Thousands and thousands of children were bused to this location to meet Wyland and Spouty (Wyland's 7 1/2 ft. tall baby sperm whale) to learn the art of saving whales. Each day Wyland and Maris Sidenstecker of Save the Whales, spent time with these school children to explain why he was painting their city a mural and the importance of water conservation whether you live on a coast line or in a land locked city like Indianapolis. Orcas Passage has to be one of the most beautiful of all Wyland's murals. Set within a Pacific Northwest seascape, the viewer is left with the feeling that he himself has actually seen the sun set over the Pacific Ocean. Featuring a huge pod of nine orca whales in green waters with a landscape of pine trees and golden sunset rays, Wyland has created a very serene and peaceful feel to a previously very boring, lifeless wall. The work of art also includes playful sea otters, sea lions, and a harbor porpoise frolicking just off the coastline while a gorgeous bald eagle soars through the northern skies. [14]

Wholesale District and Downtown Photo List and Sources

1. Introduction - www.indy.org

2. Indianapolis Circle Theater
    [2] www.indianapolissymphony.org
    [2a] Mural painted by Clifton Wheeler is being restored. Indianapolis News, Oct. 2, 1984 p.24, c.6

3. The Runners - Jim McQuiston 7 E. Washington Street 1975-76
    [3] Suzanne Rollins Stanis, Historic Landmarks Foundation

4. Urban Wall - Roland Hobart, Delaware across from City County Building, just north of Washington St.
    [4] By Marion Simon Garmel, Indianapolis News. Aug. 31, 1973

5. - 10. International Welcome Walls Carol Tharp Perrin 1999. Pennsylvania St. near
    Conseco Field house at 125 S. Pennsylvania
    Urban Walls (Delaware near Conseco)
    [5] Statement from her webpage: http://www.pbase.com/tpgartists/murals
    [6] Statements from interview with Carol Tharp-Perrin
11. - 12.5. Circle Center Mall
    [11-12a] January 13, 1999 Ruth Mullen Staff Writer Indianapolis Star (small picture)

13.-14. Wyland Mural Indianapolis Public Schools Building 120 E. Walnut 1997
    [13-14] Wyland website.

FOUNTAIN SQUARE DISTRICT

Only a mile and a half from downtown Indianapolis *Fountain Square* is located at the intersection of Virginia Avenue at Prospect and Shelby Streets. *Fountain Square* takes you back in time with original architecture that now houses antique shops, art galleries, studios, and restaurants lining the streets that lead to the fountain in the square.

Fountain Square was the first commercial historic district in Indiana. Its existing buildings span more than a century of development from 1871 to the present. Fountain Square played an important part in the Indianapolis Theater heritage; the area's commercial district had more operating theaters than could be found in any part of Indianapolis from 1910 to 1950. [1]

The Fountain Square Theatre Building opened in 1928 as a place for entertainment, shopping and professional offices until its decline began in the late 1960's. After undergoing restoration started in 1993, the building once again houses entertainment in the Fountain Square Theater, duckpin bowling in either of two vintage alleys, overnight accommodations, an original 50's soda fountain and diner, a contemporary cafe and a variety of independent shops.

Fountain Square is once again becoming an entertainment and arts destination. For more information on the Fountain Square area and its merchants visit the Fountain Square Main Street website. [2]

Fig. 2-2 **Old Billboard on top of the Fountain Square Diner Building**

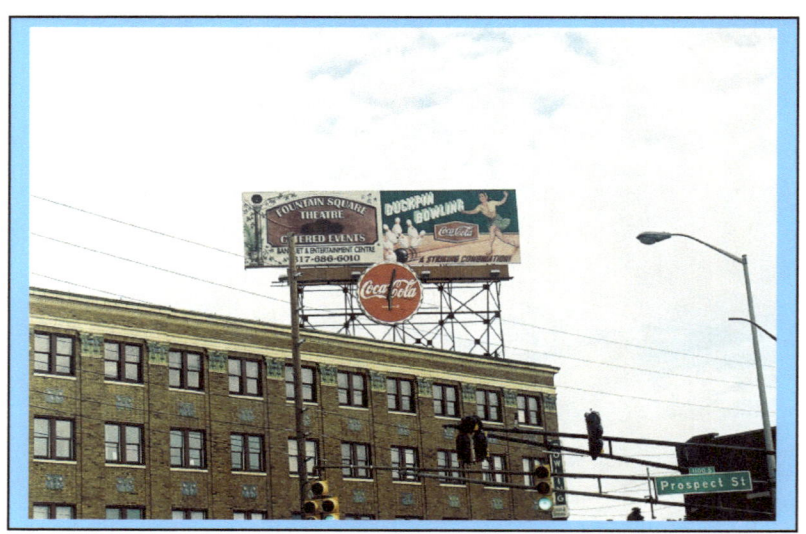

Fig. 2-3 **Classic Architecture Mural** 10 ft. High by 100 ft. long - Side of Fountain Square Theater Building 1127 Prospect Ave. Carol Tharp-Perrin

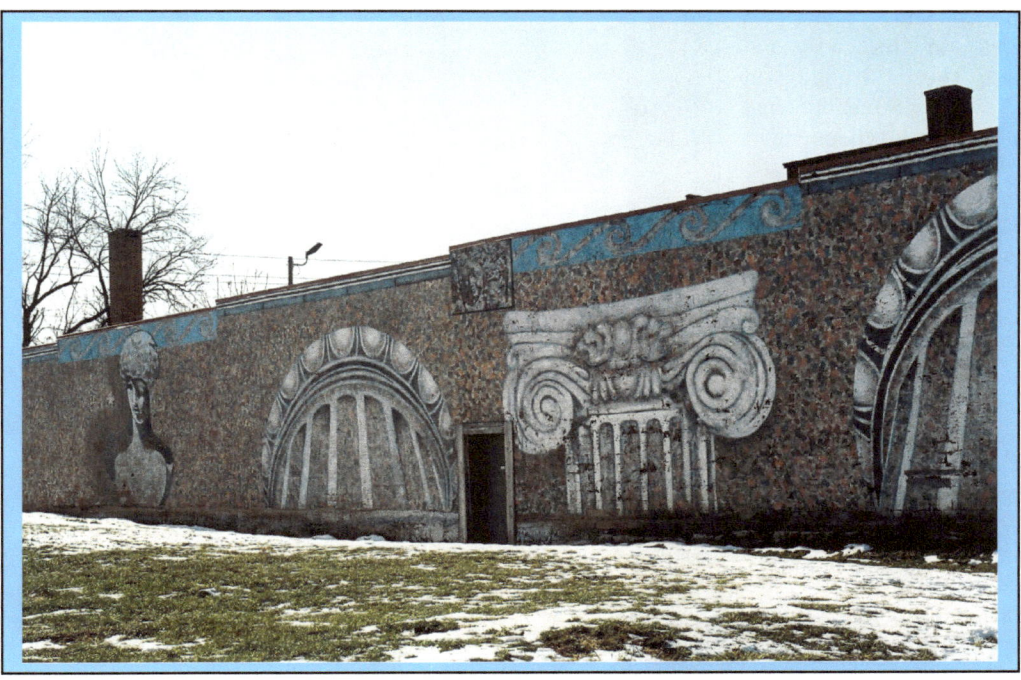

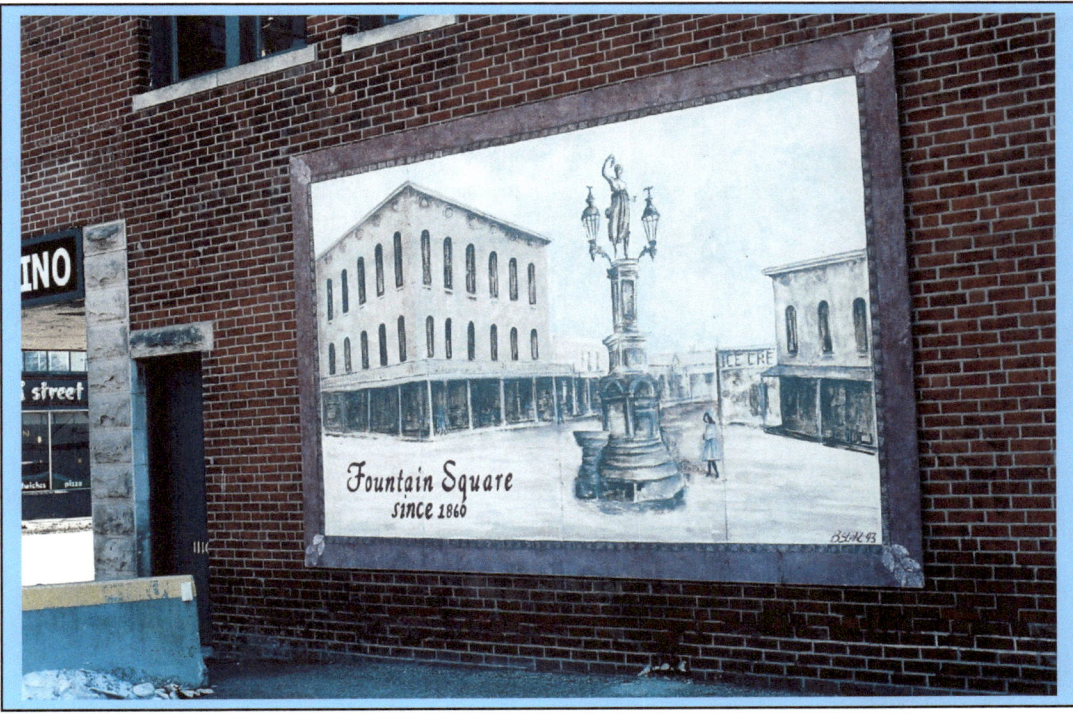

Fig. 2-4 **Fountain Square Mural** Barbara Stahl 1993 Dino's Vino at Fountain Square Intersection of Virginia, Prospect and Shelby

Fig. 2-5 **Fountain Diner Mural**

The Fountain Diner is located in the Fountain Square Theatre Building at 1103 Shelby Street in what was once the luncheonette of the F.W. Woolworth store. After the Fountain Square Theatre closed in 1959, Woolworth's occupied the ground floor of the building until it also closed in the late 1960's. The space then housed a variety of other businesses including an office furniture store and a thrift shop until it was renovated in 1994 as part of the restoration of the Fountain Square Theatre Building. The diner was reopened using the original soda fountain, grills, counter

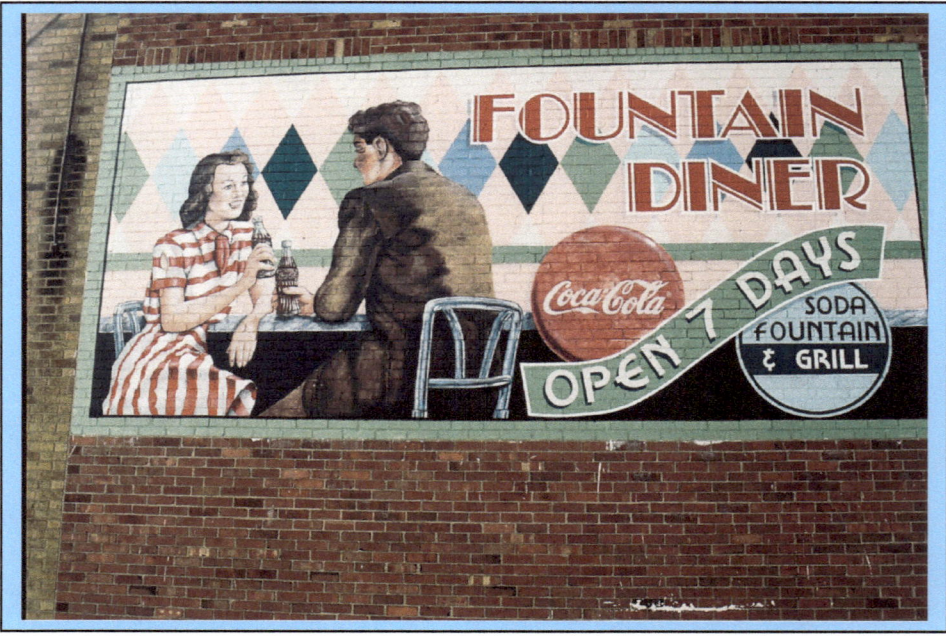

and stools obtained from another local Woolworth's store that closed in 1994. The pink, green and blue mosaic tile background is original to the space as well as the diamond motif that runs along the grill area. Today the Fountain Diner serves hand patted burgers with krinkle kut fries, jumbo tenderloins and hand dipped shakes and malts that have been voted "Best in Indy" by the Indianapolis Monthly magazine. The breakfast menu is served anytime. [5]

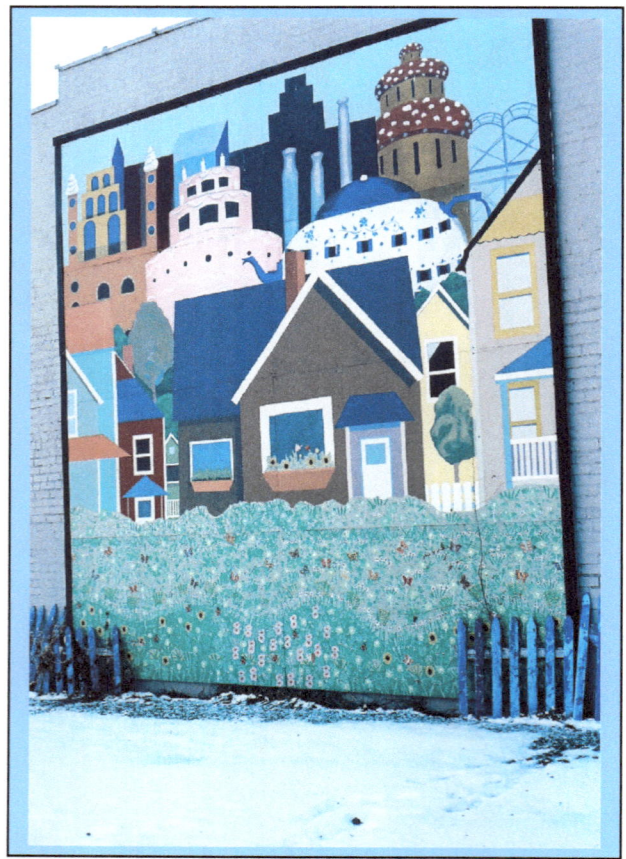

Fig. 2-6 **Village Mural**

Pedigo Jewelers, corner of Virginia and Woodlawn
Patricia Wildhack did the neighborhood scene in Fountain Square with money from weeds to seed with Bernadette Ostracovich and William Lawson and kids from a neighborhood camp. She also did the murals under the Ohio street bridge of a beach and cyclone and fields, and laundry blowing in the wind, representing scenes from southern Indiana to Northern Indiana. It was painted around 1998-99 with kids from the Shortridge magnet program. And she painted one on the Firehouse on Alabama and 16th street. This mural is on the side of Pedigo Jewelry Store at Virginia and Woodlawn.

Fig. 2-7 **Indy Murals,** back of Wheeler Arts Building
Suzy Salaz and Keenan-Stahl Boys and Girls Club, and children from Mar Elias, Israel who were in Indianapolis for an exchange program in connection with the University of Indianapolis's program at the Wheeler Arts Center. 1035 Sanders St. Indianapolis 46203.

The Wheeler Center artists are also working with senior citizens to paint a mural which will be installed in the Fountain Square Center using old photographs and their memories of Fountain Square

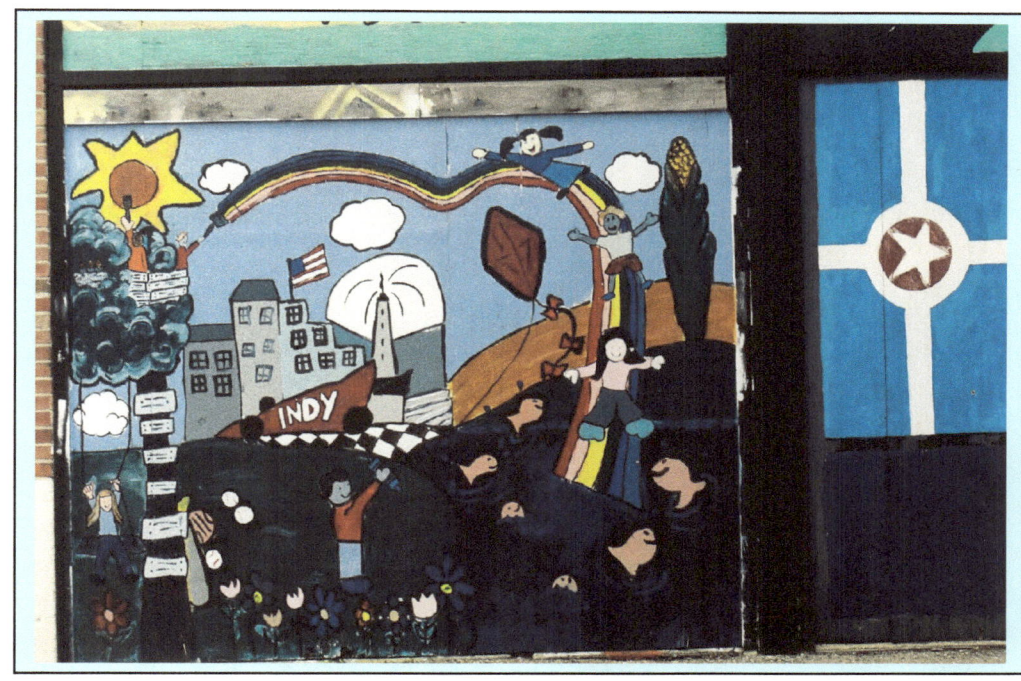

The CDC's (Community Development Corporations) also help this community. Through a mixture of federal, charitable and private money, about $20 million a year, the CDC's patch together financing for projects whose aim is to make communities safer and more stable through home ownership. These neighborhood-based groups have been embraced by the city's past two mayors as vehicles for "wealth building"—the construction of new homes and the luring of retailers to prop up the city's stagnant tax base—in declining neighborhoods. The city steers much of it $18 million in annual federal grant money for community development through the CDC's, giving them an unusual amount of financial clout for neighborhood organizations. The CDC's also act as a bulwark against the abandonment of homes. Diversity is a key goal." [7]

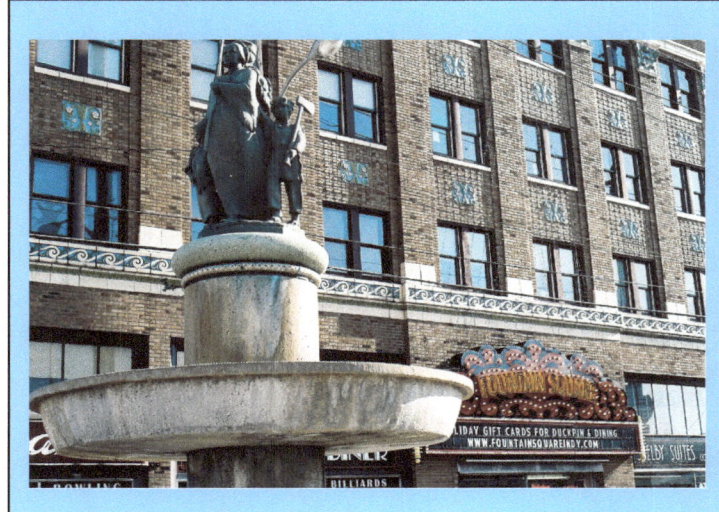

Fig. 2-8 **Fountain Square Fountain**
Fountain Square has been home to several fountains.

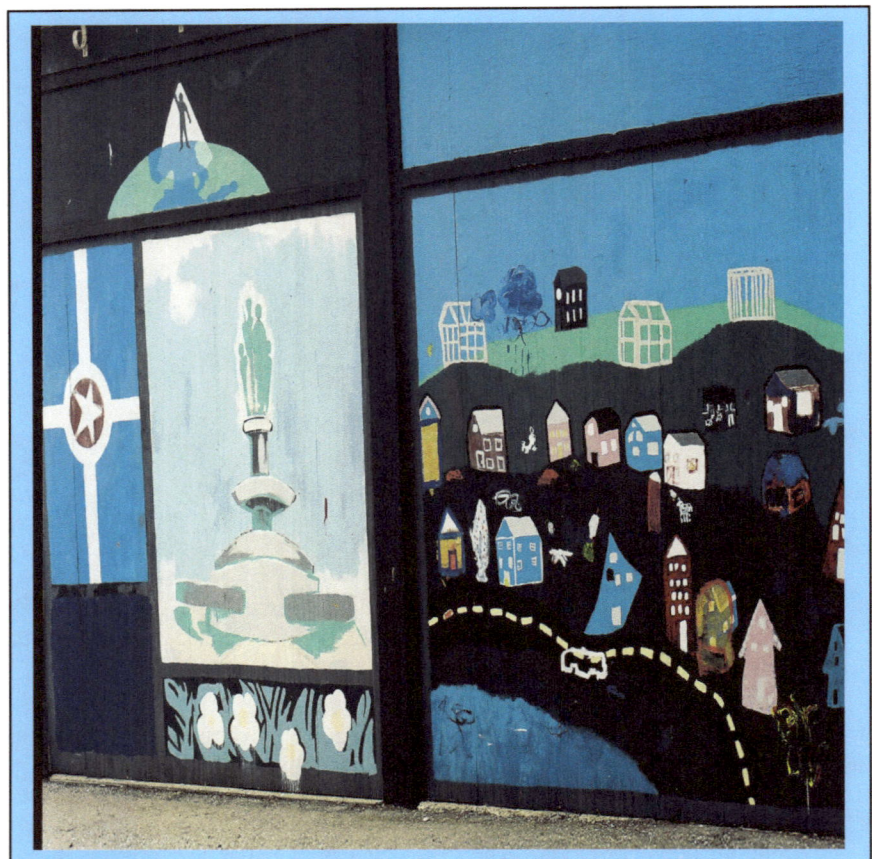

Fig. 2-9 **Wheeler Arts Building Mural** - Other side
The district was placed on the National Register of Historic Places in 1983.

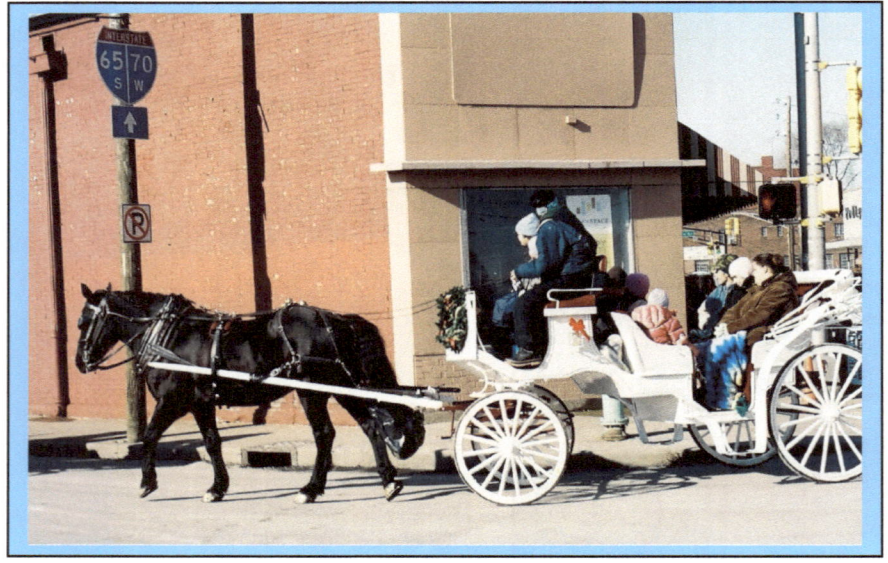

Fig. 2-10 **Carriage rides at Fountain Square - winter 2006.**

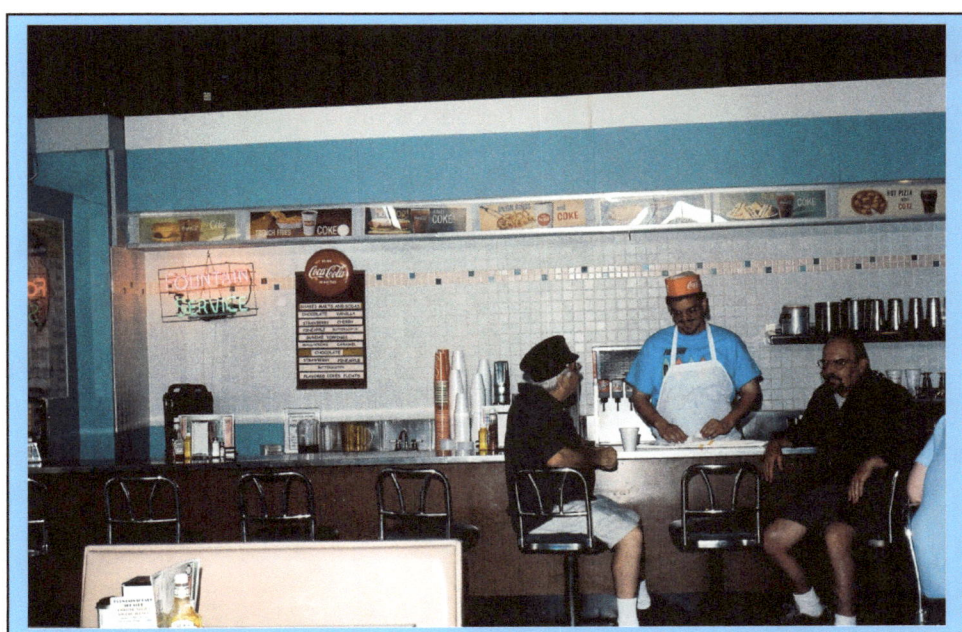

Fig. 2-11 **Old soda fountain in the Fountain Square Diner Building**

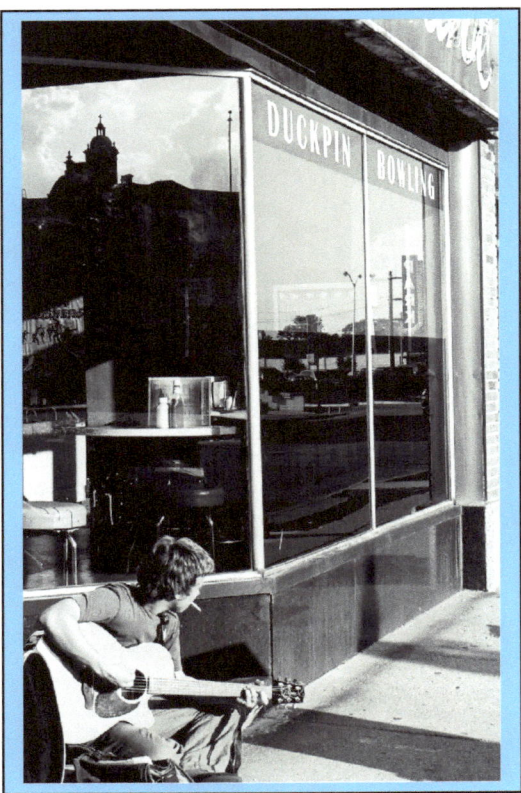

Fig. 2-12 **Guitarist and Duck Pin Bowling**
This musician was playing in front of the soda fountain on a summer morning.

The Duck Pin Bowling alley (page 21) is in the Fountain square building. The game was born in Baltimore, Maryland in 1900 and it was one of Babe Ruth's favorite games! Ten-pin bowling used to strictly be a winter sport and most alleys closed during the summer except for a few that remained open to play odd bowling games using the smaller balls. Summer bowlers suggested that it might be interesting to trim the standard pins down to match the size of the small ball. Because it was much harder to get strikes and spares, the rules were changed to allow three bowls on each turn but only counted as a score of ten if all ten pins were knocked down with the third ball. Duckpins became so popular that during the 1920's duckpin bowling spread along the east coast, from New England to Georgia. Today duckpin houses are still found only in the eastern states with the exception of our location here in Fountain Square. [12]

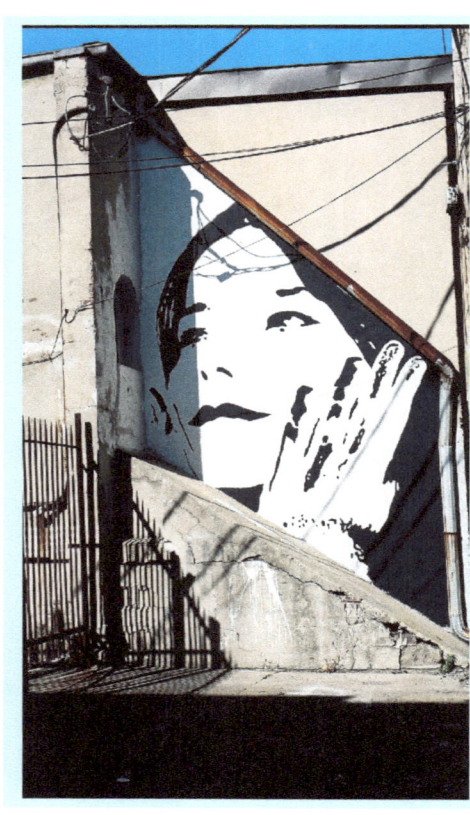

Fig. 2-13 **Face -** Alley behind buildings on Virginia Avenue between Shelby and Woodlawn.

Fig. 2-14 **Free Period** Quote on yellow door says, "The aim of public education is not to spread enlightenment at all. It is simply to reduce as many individuals as possible to the same safe level; to breed a standard citizenry to put down dissent and originality. H. L. Mencken

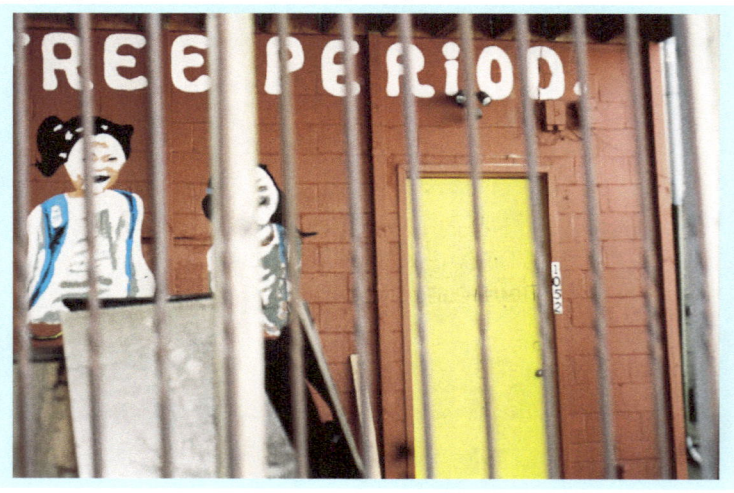

Fig. 2-15 **Be Independent -** Primo, WDR 07, VIC, Liber - Alley behind buildings on Virginia Avenue between Shelby and Woodlawn.

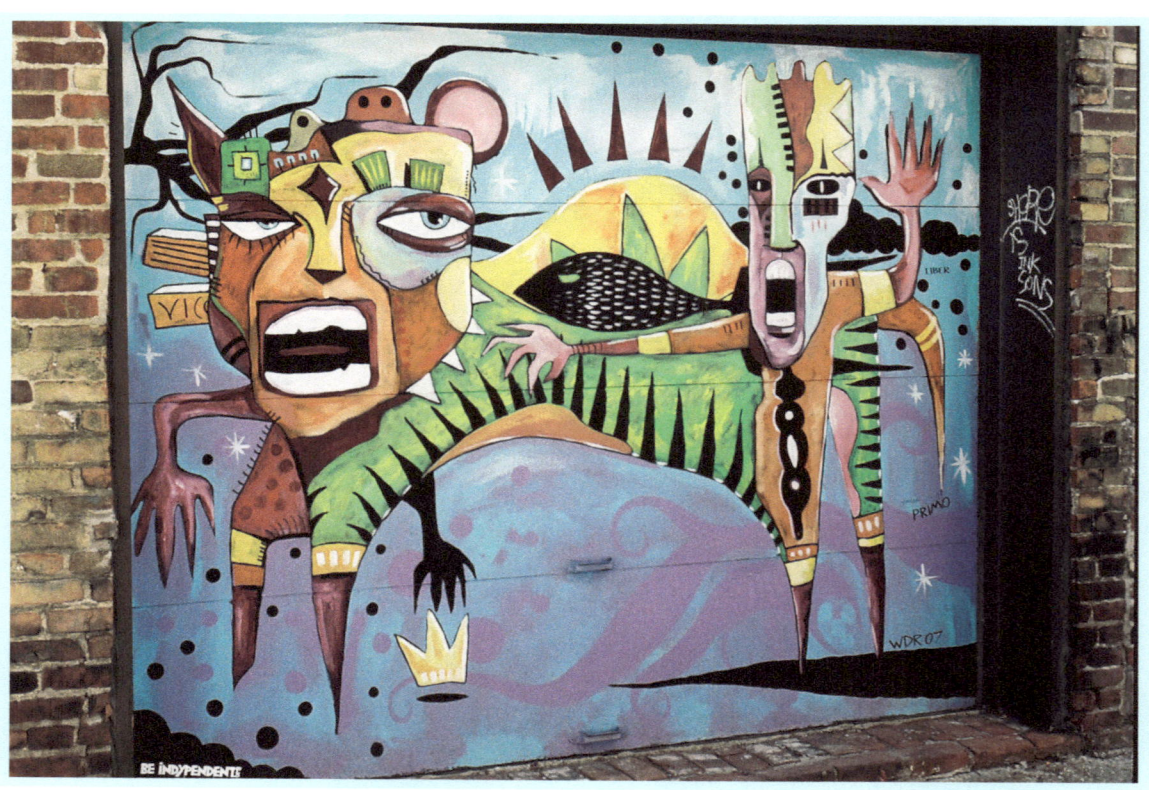

Figs. 2-16 and 17 **Indy.com and IConsume** (same location as previous)
The quote on IConsume says, "The goals of Corporate Consumerism require that we fail to seek better alternatives. That we fail even to see the existence of a problem to be solved. That we live according to an entirely inadequate sense of values. That we suffer and, if necessary, die for profit. " David Edwards

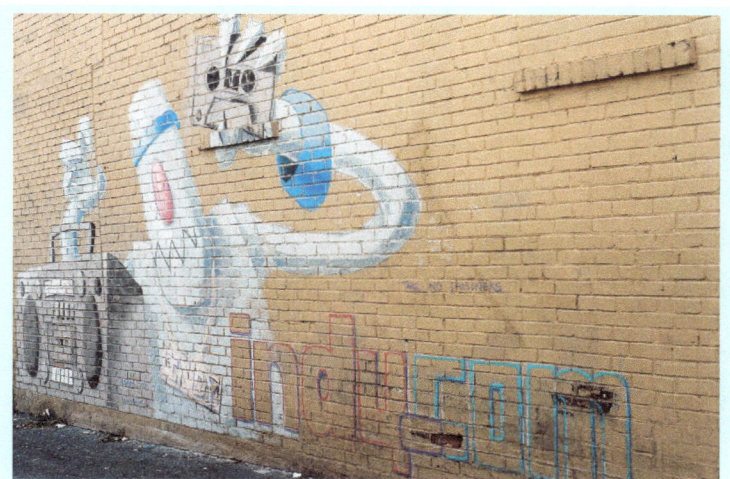
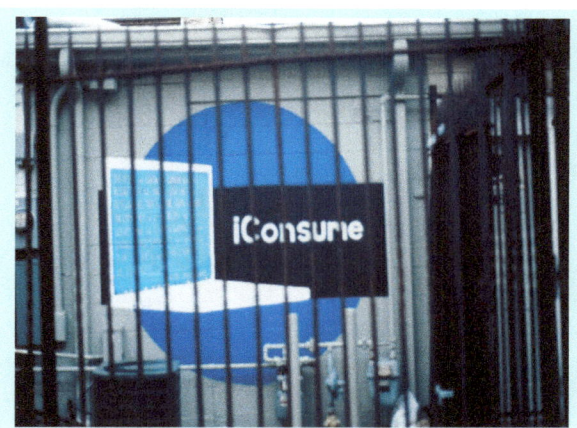

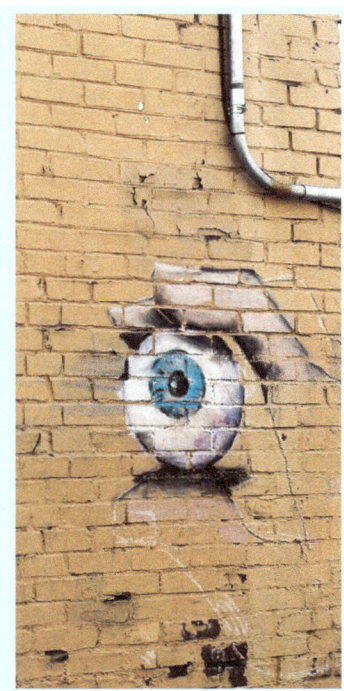
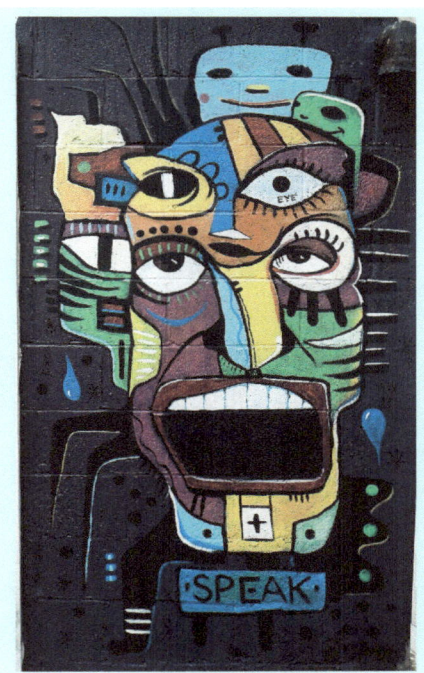

Fig. 2-18 **EYEBALL** Same alley.　　　　　　Fig. 2-19 **SPEAK** Same alley

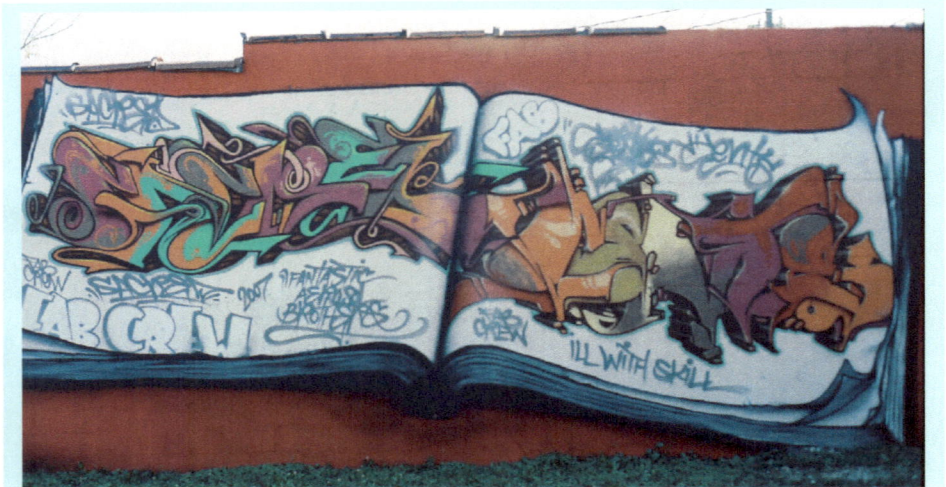

Fig. 2-20 **Fab Crew, ILL with Skill** Santorini's Restaurant parking lot, 1417 Prospect

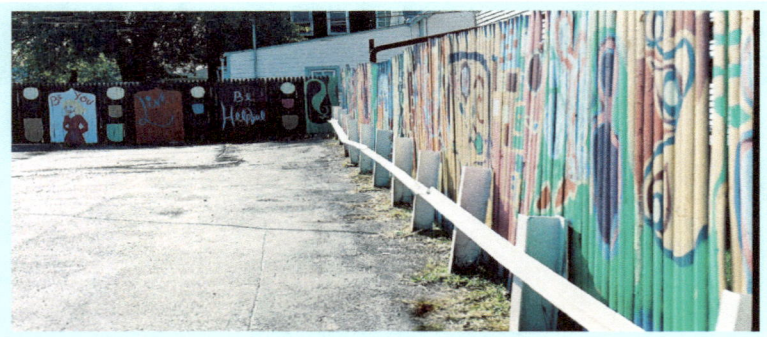

Fig. 2-21 **Fence around Santorini's** Greek Restaurant **parking lot**.

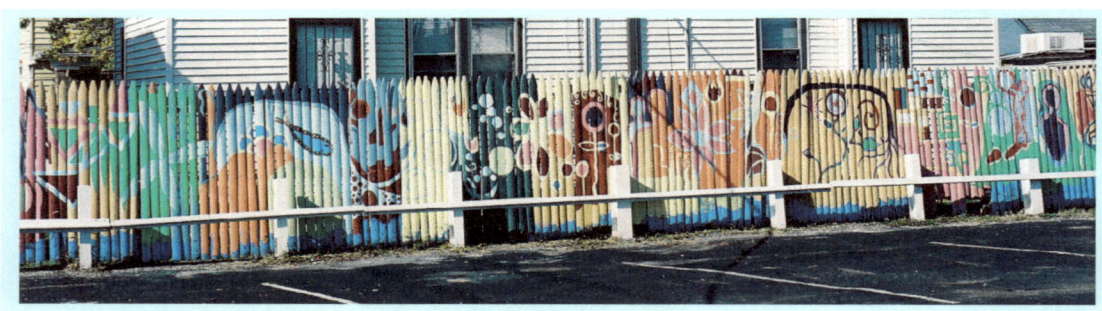

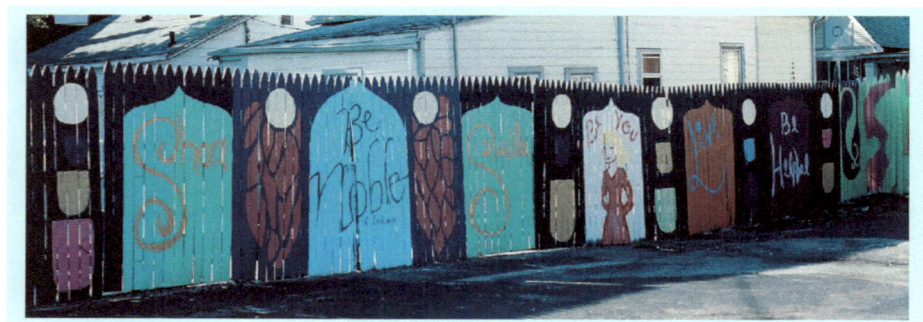

Fig. 2-22, 23 **Fence around Santorini's parking lot.**

Fountain Square Photo List and Sources

1. Intro - © Copyright 2001 Fountain Square
2. Old Billboard on top of the Fountain Square Diner Building.
   [2] info@fountainsquareindy.com
3. Architecture Mural - Carol Tharp-Perrin 1127 Prospect Ave.
4. Fountain Square Mural, Barbara Stahl, 1991, Fountain Square
5. Fountain Square Mural, 1103 Shelby Street
   [5] | info@fountainsquareindy.com
6. Village Mural, Pedigo Jewelry Store, Virginia and Woodlawn, Patricia Wildhack
7. Indy Murals - Wheeler Arts building
   Back of Wheeler Arts Building. Suzy Salaz and Keenan-Stahl Boys and Girls Club, and children from Mar Elias, Israel who were in Indianapolis for an exchange program in connection with the University of Indianapolis's program at the Wheeler Arts Center. 1035 Sanders St. Indianapolis 46203.
   [7]Conscientious investors helping fight the blight – Community revitalization. April 21, 2002 Indy Star
   Author: Doug Sword
8. Fountain Square Fountain
9. Other side of the Wheeler Arts Building Mural
10. Carriage in 2006
11. Old soda fountain in the Fountain Square Diner Building
12. Guitarist in front of Fountain Square Building
13.-19. Murals in alley behind buildings on Virginia Avenue between Shelby and Woodlawn
20.-23 Murals in Santorini's Greek Restaurant parking lot. 1417 Prospect
24. Duck Pin Bowling – Fountain Square Diner Building at intersection of Shelby,
    Prospect and Virginia Avenue.
    [24] info@fountainsquareindy.com

Fig. 2-24

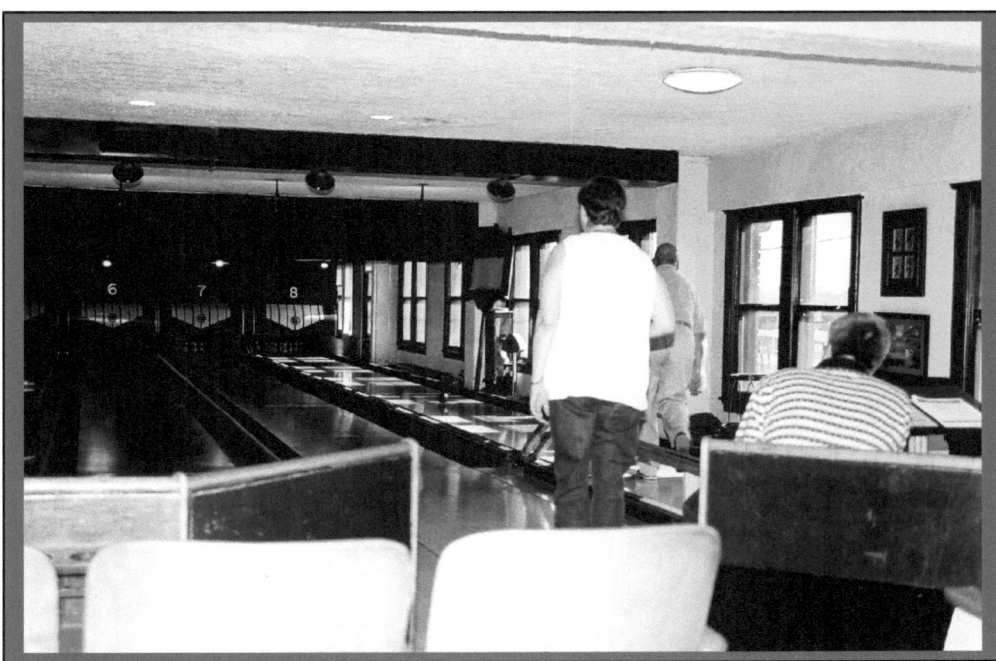

Just a few blocks northeast of Monument Circle lies Downtown Indianapolis' world-renowned Arts District. Massachusetts Avenue, more commonly called Mass Ave. was one of the original diagonal streets in Indianapolis. Today, more than seven blocks are filled with galleries, restaurants, theatres, and unique owner-operated shops. It is one of the original angled streets in Indianapolis, thus the Indianapolis cultural districts guide's "45 degrees from the ordinary" designation. [1]

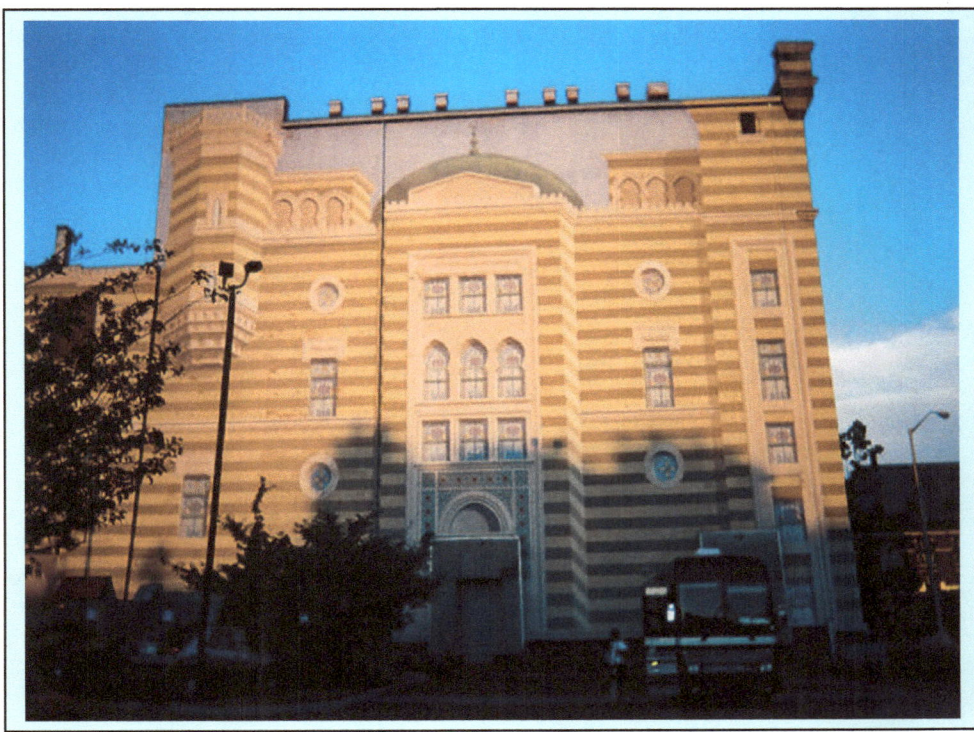

Fig 3-2 **Murat Temple, West Side** 510 N. New Jersey St., Indianapolis, IN Several murals: Middle East Scene (outside north) There is also an Egyptian Tomb/Oasis Mural inside and this16,000 foot mural on west wall outside. Date: 1968 (tile-opposite) 1990's (west wall) Media: Tiles (north), paint (west wall) Artist: Many different artists including, S.D. Battista (who restored the Oasis painting inside) and Jeff Greene and Indianapolis resident Mike Bennett.   EverGreene Studios of New York City for renovation and outside west wall done in the mid 1990's. [2]

Fig. 3-3 **North side of Murat Temple**, 510 N. New Jersey St., Indianapolis, IN. This mural depicts a Middle East scene that refers to activities of the Shriners in the Murat or the Mosque of the Ancient Arabic Order of the Nobles of the Mystic Shrine. The temple itself, Shrinedom's 17th, was chartered in June 1884. It was expanded in 1909 to include the theater, and in 1923 to house the Egyptian, social and banquet rooms. A final addition, from 1969, accommodates the Shrine Club. The building is expansive with many hiding places. The exotic ambience of the Egyptian Room, with its murals depicting the glories of King Tut's Egypt, adds to its mysticism.

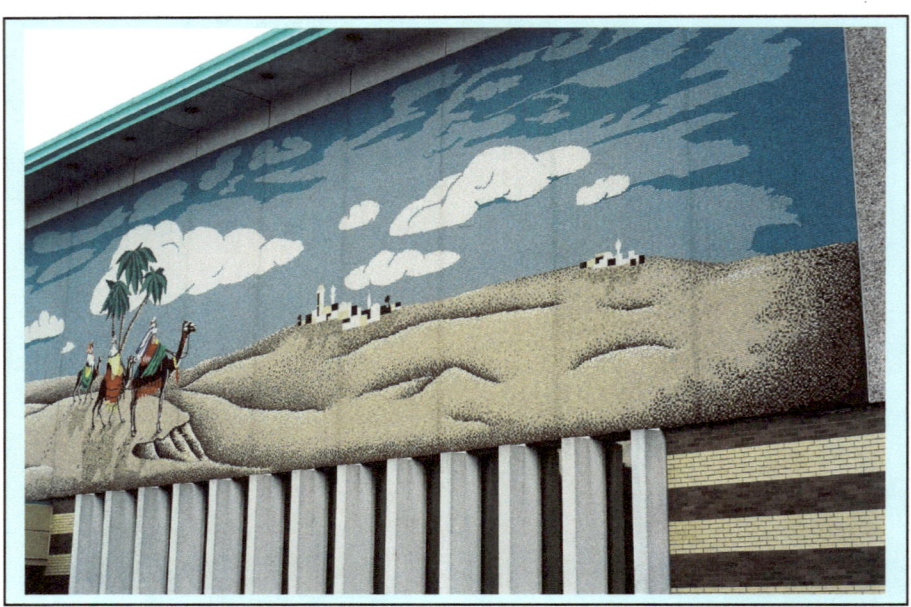

It was renovated in the mid 1990's when the mural was painted on the outside wall. Touted by mayor (Goldsmith) as gateway to Mass Ave. [3]

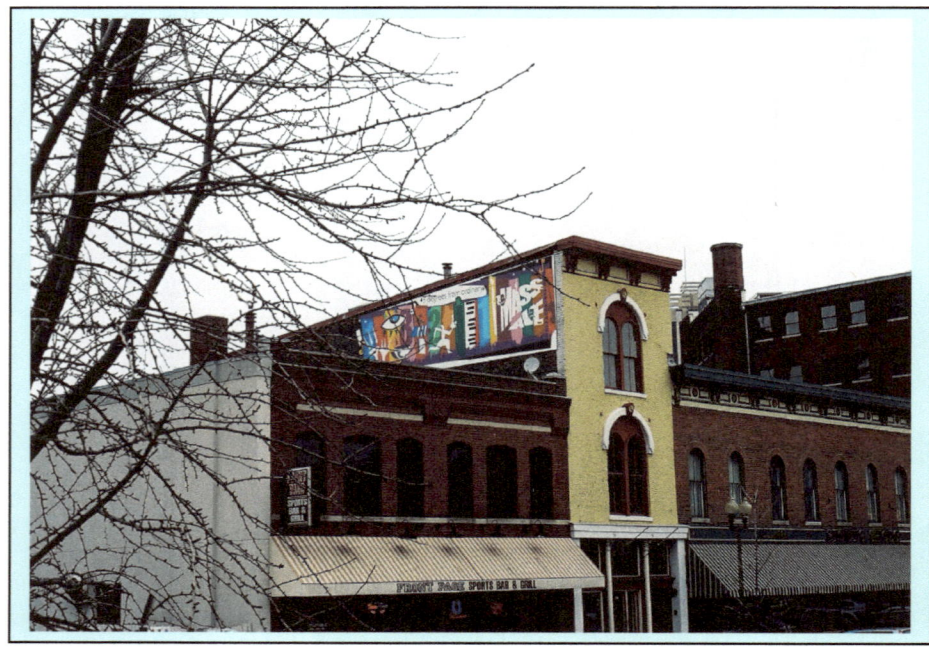

Fig. 3-4 **The "gateway"** project is just one element of the cultural district effort being underwritten by the city's Cultural Development Commission. In the Mass Ave Arts & Theatre District, other projects have included the installation of nine art display cases that not only show the works of local artists, but also feature calendar items to let people know what else is happening on the Avenue. The initiative is also responsible for the Mass Ave "window statics" seen in many merchants' windows; the sidewalk applications that are also designed to remind visitors they are in the Mass Ave Arts & Theatre District; a website www.discovermassave.com and a comprehensive district guide.[4] One mural adorns the top of the building at 314 Mass Ave, (Stouts Shoe Store) easily visible to motorists headed northbound on Delaware Street or eastbound on New York Street.

Fig. 3-5 **Gateway Mural**
The other installation hangs on the north face of The Chatterbox Jazz Club, clearly visible to motorists passing by on busy Michigan Street. Both installations were designed by Indianapolis artist William Denton Ray and installed by Expo Design.
A third installation commissioned for the East End of Mass Ave is clearly visible from the interstate. [5]

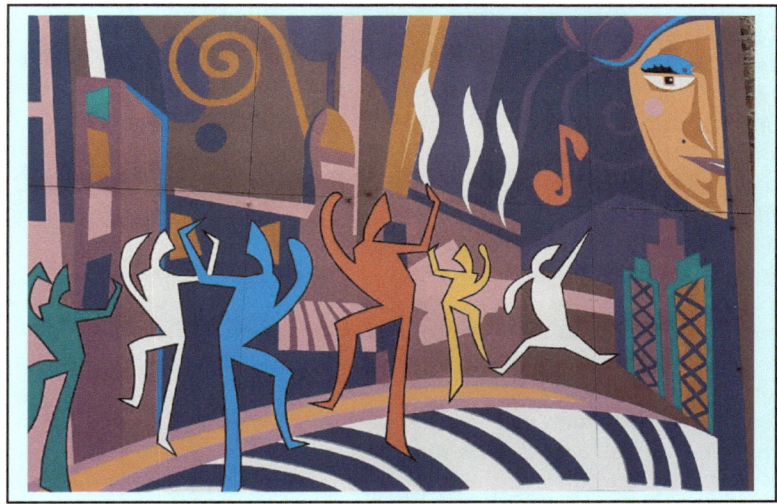

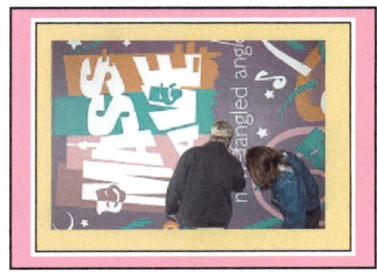

Fig. 3-6 **Artist William Denton Ray** looks over his work with Susan Vogt of Riley Area Development Corp., who coordinated the gateway effort for the Mass Ave Arts & Theater District. [6]

Fig. 3-7 **Gateway Mural,** Christopher Blice and Jonathan Edwards
The final mural in a series of three Mass Ave visual "gateways" is on the side of a building at 911 Massachusetts Ave. Drivers traveling south on I-65 will have the best view of the 3-D mural, which depicts the Mass Ave cultural district logo incorporated with a picture frame, stage lights and a ramp-jumping bicyclist. **Christopher Blice**, who designed the mural with **Jonathan Edwards** of Blice Edwards Studios, says the 26-foot-by-15-foot-by-2-1/2-foot mural has been painted on metal.

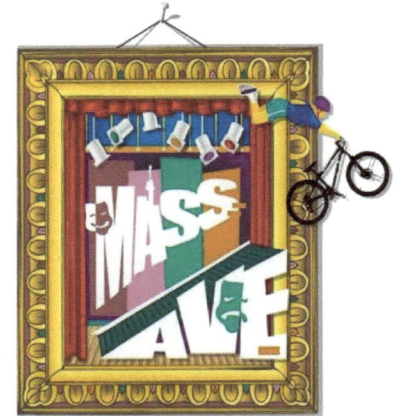

"We were going to do it on canvas," Blice says. "But we thought about it being weathered and not lasting very long -- maybe five years. On metal, it will probably last 100 years." The building at 911 Massachusetts Ave. currently is home to businesses such as The Bike Line. In the late 1990s, a "Bob and Tom Show" mural painted on the building was deemed illegal, according to sign regulations enforced by the Department of Metropolitan Development.
The mural joins other Mass Ave wall paintings on the side of the Chatterbox Jazz Club, 435 Massachusetts Ave., and Stout's Shoes, 314 Massachusetts Ave. [7]

Fig. 3-8 and 9 **Ghost Signs**

Massachusetts Avenue was lined with shops in the 40's and then fell victim to urban blight in the 70's and was then known for its pawn shops and junk stores, except for the famous Stout's shoes. Founded in 1886 with its parrot named Billy and its antique shoe delivery system of unusual wire baskets on cables with pulleys to take the money and return the wrapped package to the customer. Stouts has yet to experience a robbery.

In the 70's Mass Ave. was called "Little Hellhole". My grandmother and I used to venture into the cavernous junk stores to find treasures or junk. It was the epitome of "Skid Row" with its derelict buildings, seedy bars, drunken bums sleeping in doorways and endless parade of prostitutes after dark. In the early 1980's the downtown Renaissance began. Now the area literally crackles with energy around the clock. Hungry diners pack the restaurants, art lovers frequent the galleries, and theater lovers hurry to attend Theater on the Square, the Atheneum or Murat. [8]

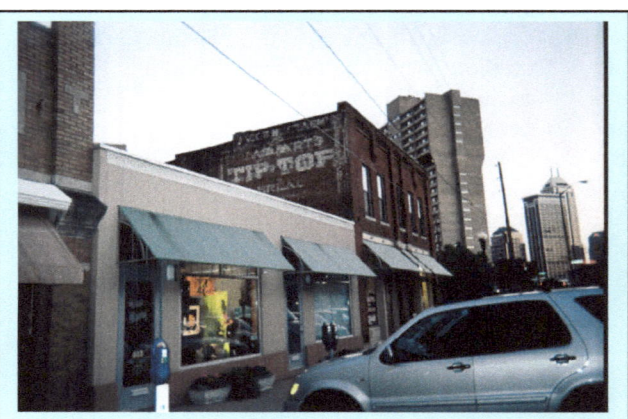

The text in Italics above is taken from "Little Hellhole" to Cultural Showcase by P.R. Parker. Copyright © 2005 by P.R. Parker. All Rights Reserved

Tip Top Bread was known for issuing Pittsburgh Pirates baseball cards in the 40's and of course Quaker Oats was the "work food". [8a]

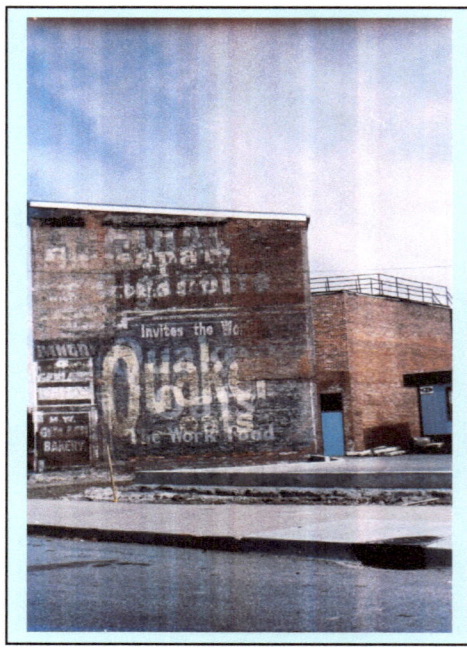

Fig. 3-9 **Quaker Oats**
Massachusetts Ave.

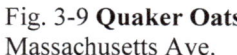

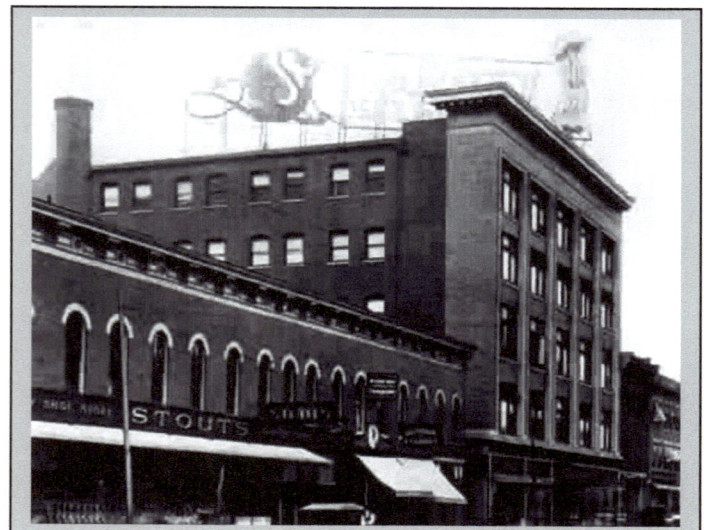

Fig. 3-10 **Photograph – Indiana Historical Society Title** Stouts Shoe Store, Marott Department Store, Massachusetts Avenue, 1909 (Bass #310579-4)

Item ID folder165_doc79.jpg
Subject Buildings. **Box/Folder** Box 18, Folder 4
Creator W. H. Bass Photo Company
Geographic Location Indiana--Indianapolis
Format of Original Photographic print, b&w
Digital Format JPG
Owning Institution Indiana Historical Society
Collection Name W. H. Bass Photo Company Collection **Collection Number** P 0130 **Type** Image **Copyright Notice** Digital image © 2004 Indiana Historical Society. All Rights Reserved. [10]

The **Indiana Avenue Cultural District** encompasses the most historically rich commercial district for Indianapolis' African American community. The area is known for history, music, restored neighborhoods and spirituality. See chapter on Labor, Race Relations, Politics and Patriotism for a historical discussion and their website at http://www.discoverindianaavenue.com/."

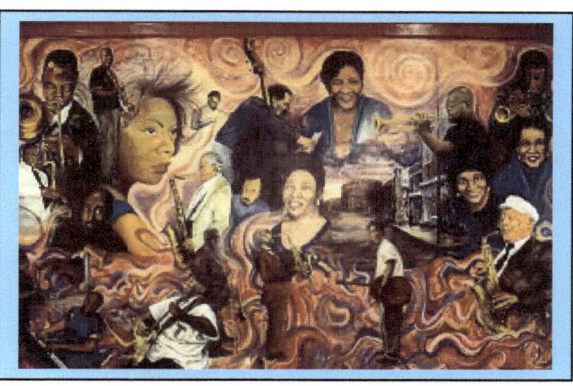

Fig.3-11 **The "Street of Dreams"** Indy Parks, Watkins Family Center, 2360 Martin Luther King Blvd., Indianapolis, IN 46204 Although this mural is not technically in the Indiana Ave. cultural district, it located nearby and "right on" in subject matter.

One hundred fifth grade students from neighborhood Indianapolis Public Schools 42,44 and 87 collaborated with professional artists and musicians to create the abstract linear rhythms of this mural. Then these painted rhythms were developed into an overall design that featured musicians who played out their dreams from Indiana Avenue - a birthplace of jazz. All of the musicians in the mural can be identified and some include J. J. Johnson, David Baker, Flo Garvin Deakyne, Virgil Jones, Cheryl Hayes, Mary Moss, Jimmy McDaniels, Wes Montgomery and Jimmy Coe. There are 22 musicians pictured and a plaque beside the mural identifies them. Carol Tharp-Perrin, Barbara Stahl, Larry Gindhart and others. (See Labor, Race Relations, Politics and Patriotism , V. 1 for full discussion) [11]

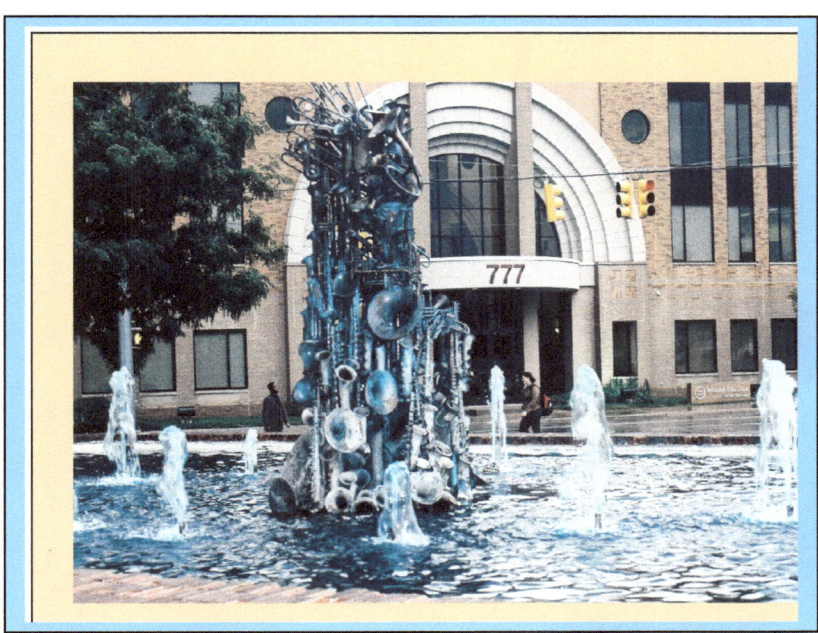

Fig. 3-12 **Sculpture of musical instruments on Indiana Avenue** in front of the restored Lockfield Garden apartments.

By John Spaulding whose father, James, was a 1930s jazz guitarist.. The work, Jammin' on the Avenue, is a collage of brass musical instruments welded together in a vertical column, namely saxophones, trumpets, sousaphones and trombones. [12]

Fig. 13-14 **Madame C.J. Walker** As a manufacturer of hair care products for African American women, Madame C. J. Walker, born Sarah Breedlove, became one of the first American women millionaires.

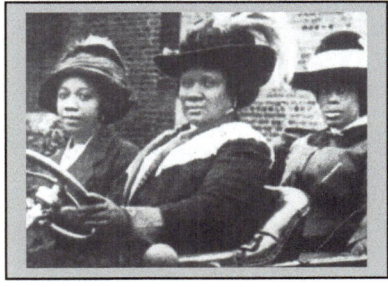

The Madame Walker Theater is in the Indiana Ave. Cultural District at 617 Indiana Avenue, Indianapolis, IN 46202 in the Madame C.J. Walker Building.

*I am a woman who came from the cotton fields of the South. From there I was promoted to the washtub. From there I was promoted to the cook kitchen. And from there I promoted myself into the business of manufacturing hair goods and preparations.... I have built my own factory on my own ground."*Madam Walker,
National Negro Business League Convention, July 1912

The Madame C.J. Walker Building, constructed in 1927, is internationally known as a place where arts and cultural heritage flourish. The building is on both the national and state registries as a Historic Landmark built in tribute to its namesake, Madam C.J. Walker. http://www.walkertheatre.com

Massachusetts Avenue and Indiana Avenue Photo List and Sources

1. Intro   http://www.discovermassave.com/
2. Murat Temple
    [2] Mural may mean hope for Murat Indianapolis Star, Visual Arts by Steve Mannheimer, November 12, 1995 Page 107, City Final Ed. Record No. INDY 734058
3. [3] same
4. Mass Ave. William Denton Ray
    [4] http://www.discovermassave.com/userctl.cfm?PageContentTypeID=1&PageContentID=9
5. [5] same
6. [6] same
7. Mass Ave. Gateway mural
    [7]
    http://www.bsu.edu/capic/gateways/projects/urbantimes_feb06b.pdf#search='william%20denton%20ray
8.-9. Tip Top Bread and Quaker Oats
    [8] From, "Little Hellhole" to Cultural Showcase by P.R. Parker
    http://crazedwriter.250free.com/essays/mas_ave.html)
    [8a] http://d21c.com/sugarcrisp/essays/mass_ave.html
10. Stout's Factory Shoe Store Company, Foudned:1886 Location 66-68 Massachusetts Avenue, Indianapolis (1886-)
    318 Massachusetts Avenue
    [10] http://images.indianahistory.org/fullres/DC002/volume0/P0130_244822P8.tif Stouts Shoe Store etc. (1909)
11. Indiana Jazz Mural (The Street of Dreams) in Indy Parks, Watkins Family Center, 2360 Martin Luther King Blvd., Indianapolis, IN 46204
    [10]http://www.pbase.com/tpgartists/murals
12. Sculpture "Jammin on the Avenue" by John Spaulding Near 777 Indiana Ave.
13.-14. Madame C .J. Walker http://www.madamcjwalker.com/
    Photos from http://www.richmond.k12.va.us/schools/stuart/c.j.walker.htm
                http://www.notablebiographies.com/Tu-We/Walker-Madame-C-J.html

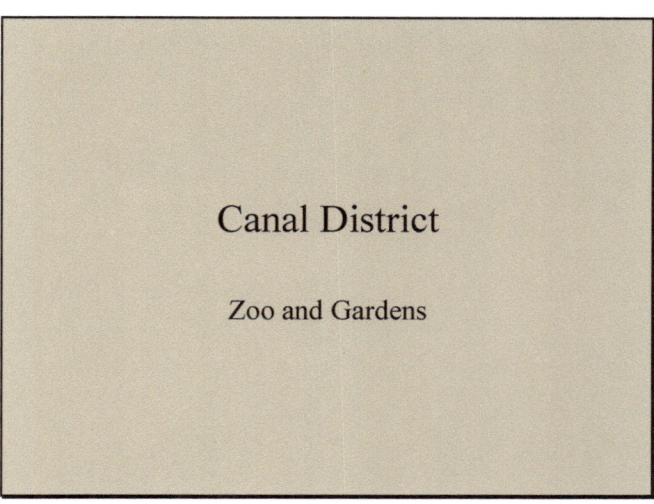

Canal District

Zoo and Gardens

Indiana's Central Canal was dug as part of the mammoth Internal Improvements Act of 1836. The Canal was part of a statewide system of man-made waterways used to enhance transportation. Unfortunately, the initiative put the state into bankruptcy and the Canal was never completed. Additionally, railroads started to become the preferred method of transportation in the 1840s. Eventually, many of the canals disappeared. The Central Canal was used until 1969, when the Downtown portion was abandoned and fell into a state of disrepair.

In the 1980s, the Downtown Canal was refurbished and reopened as a city recreational area. Venetian canals inspired this new incarnation. Gradually, cultural attractions were built along the Canal throughout the 1990s. The north end of the Canal is now home to a burgeoning bio-sciences initiative, anchored by a state-certified technology park. [1]

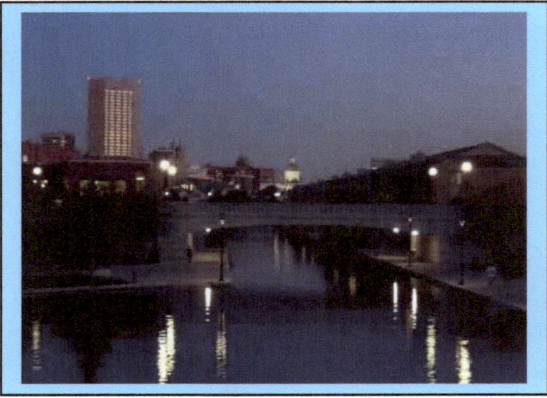

Fig. 4-2 **Canal Views** An extension of the Canal into the heart of the growing White River State Park was completed in 1996. $20,000,000 project that included renovation of the Old Washington Street Bridge, built in 1916 as part of the National Road, into a pedestrian crossing that links park attractions. Scattered throughout the Canal and 250-acre state park are the city's most inspiring museums, attractions and celebrations. Discover Indiana's heritage as you meander along the limestone walkway, enjoying a stunning backdrop of the Downtown skyline. This cultural destination boasts seven major attractions, festival space, public art, unique cafes and three miles of walkways on the refurbished historic Central Canal. [2]

Fig. 4-2a **Indianapolis Canal**

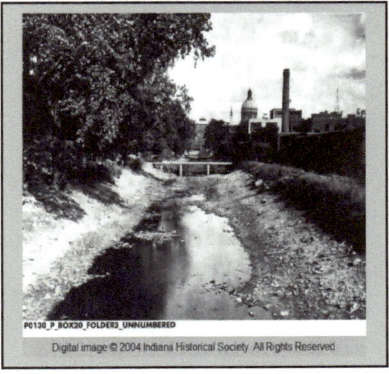

Fig 4-3 **Latinos at the Crossroads** Under the West Street canal bridge
Artist: Tony Ortega
Latinos at the Crossroads is a mural that was dedicated during a ceremony opening an exhibition of contemporary painting at the Eiteljorg Museum. The mural depicts a courtyard-like scene with several Hispanic men and women and an ancient pyramid and a lamppost that represents knowledge. Tony Ortega, one of the 19 artists, whose work was on display, took charge. He has done similar community projects in his home town of Denver. [3]

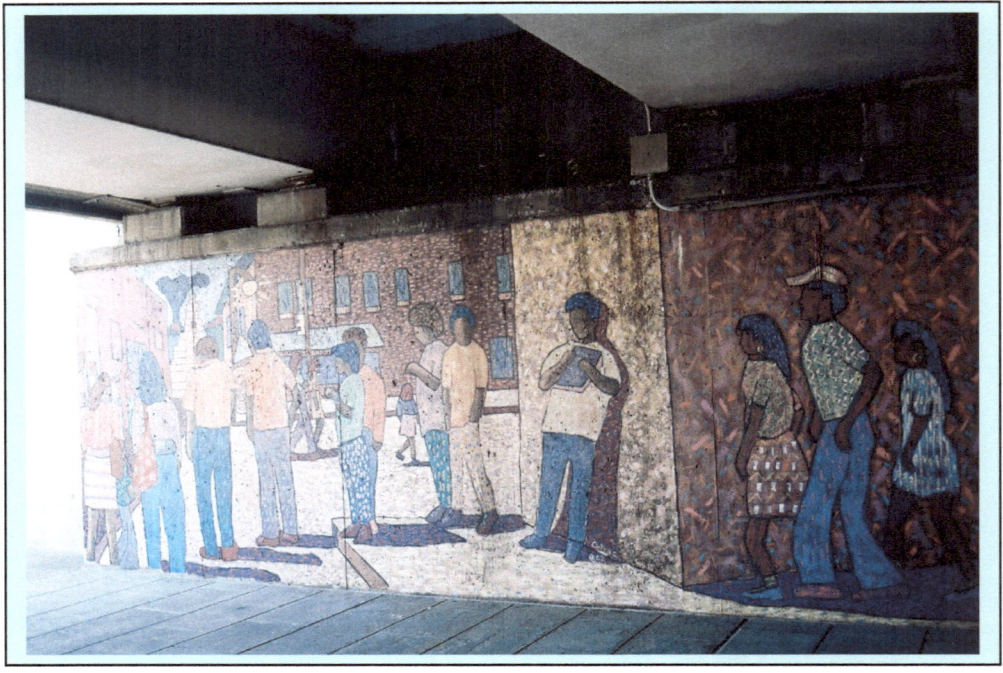

Ortega, who was paid by the Eiteljorg to create the mural, spent much of he week telling volunteers which colors and techniques to use. He did some of the painting himself. Five middle school students from the Key Learning Community arrived to help. They added dollops and dashes of festive acrylic paint, giving texture to buildings and people.
"I think it's good," said Mark McGhee, a sixth-grader enrolled in the IPS program. Samantha Pennington, an IPS assistant who watched over the students, said, "It's good for the kids to experience different cultures."

The Hispanic population increased 294 percent in Marion County to 33,290 from 1990 to 2000. [3a]

Fig. 4-4 **Goddess Mural**
Artist: Stahl Studios

The mural "Goddess" was funded by Keep Indianapolis Beautiful, Inc. as part of its Project 180 degrees/IPL Revive a Neighborhood Program and sponsored by Girls Incorporated of Indianapolis. The mural was created and directed by Stahl Studios Inc. and is 12 x 12 feet, comprised squares, and has a border of 42 12 x 12 inch squares. Each square of the border contains a girl's self portrait as a goddess of their choosing. The girls did all of the work from sanding and priming, to painting the entire mural.
The mural project began in January 2004. Its original premise was to expand on the Girls Inc. motto "Unity through Diversity" by utilizing the girls' self-portraits in the context of their ethnic heritages and humanitarian goals. [4]

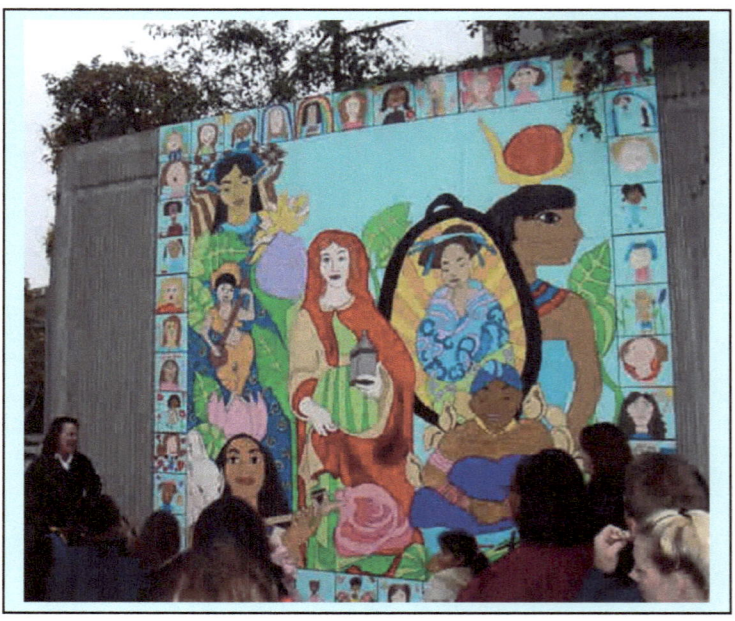

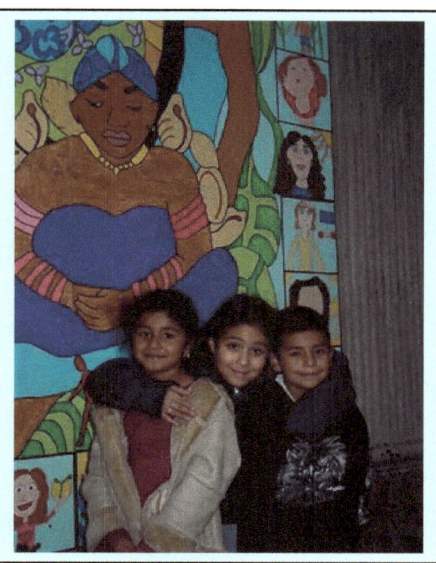

Fig. 4-5 **Goddess Mural**

Self-portraits include goddesses of
world peace, life, rainbows, peaceful sleep, education, beauty and
protectors of the children, sick, and elderly. The project took three months
to complete as part of the after school program. The mural can be seen
prominently displayed on the canal walk near the canal bridge underpass at
Ohio Street between Senate and West Streets, next to the waterfall just
south of the Ohio Street bridge. [5]
Photography by Nathan Robinson

*Girls Incorporated is a national nonprofit youth organization dedicated to
inspiring all girls to be strong, smart, and bold. With roots dating to 1864,
Girls Inc has provided vital educational programs to millions of American
girls, particularly those in high-risk, under-served areas. Today, innovative
programs help girls confront subtle societal messages about their value
and potential, and prepare them to lead successful, independent, and
fulfilling lives. [5a]*

Fig. 4-6 **Indiana Scenes**
Painted by artist Patricia Wildhack with kids from the Shortridge magnet program.
Date: 1999
Dimensions: 8 x 20 and wraps around side of bridge
Location: Under the Ohio Street Bridge
Murals represent southern and northern Indiana.

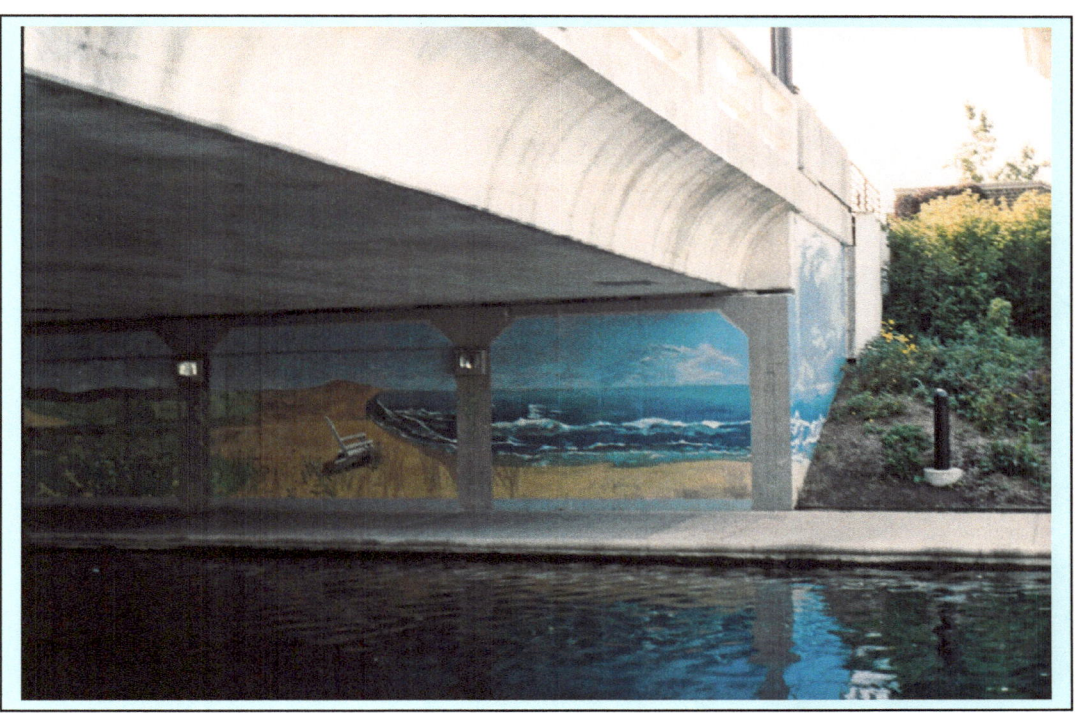

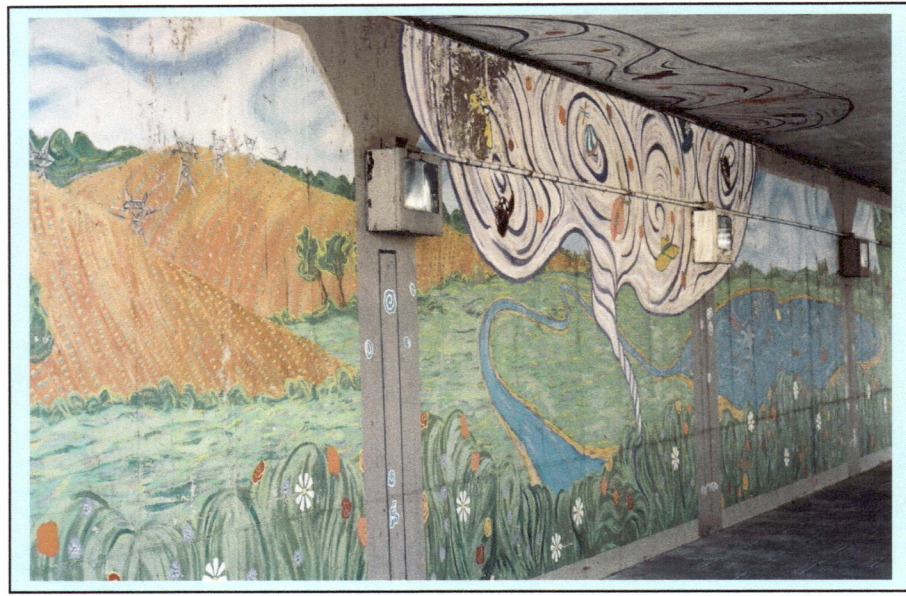

Fig. 4-7 **Ohio Street Bridge Mural**
Patricia Wildhack also painted this mural in 1998-99 with kids from the Shortridge magnet program and the one on the fire house on Alabama and 16th street. Bill Spalding was the arts center's outreach director.

Fig. 4-8 **U.S.S. Indianapolis Mural** Under the New York Street Bridge
Artist: Cynthia Walden
You can visit the U.S.S. Indianapolis Memorial in Downtown Indianapolis. This national memorial honors the crew of the Navy cruiser USS Indianapolis sunk in 1945 during World War II. Located at the north end of the Canal Walk on the east bank, it is an outdoor site open 24 hours a day. U.S.S. Indianapolis Memorial, Senate Ave & Walnut St, Indianapolis, Marion County. The mural honors the USS Indianapolis and the American flag.

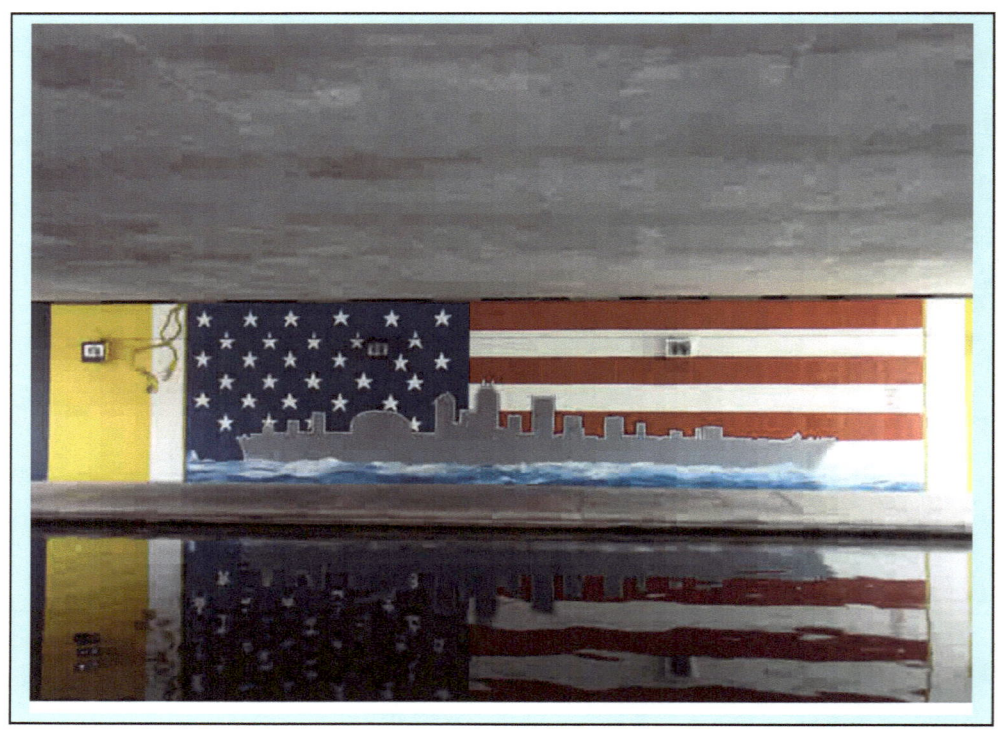

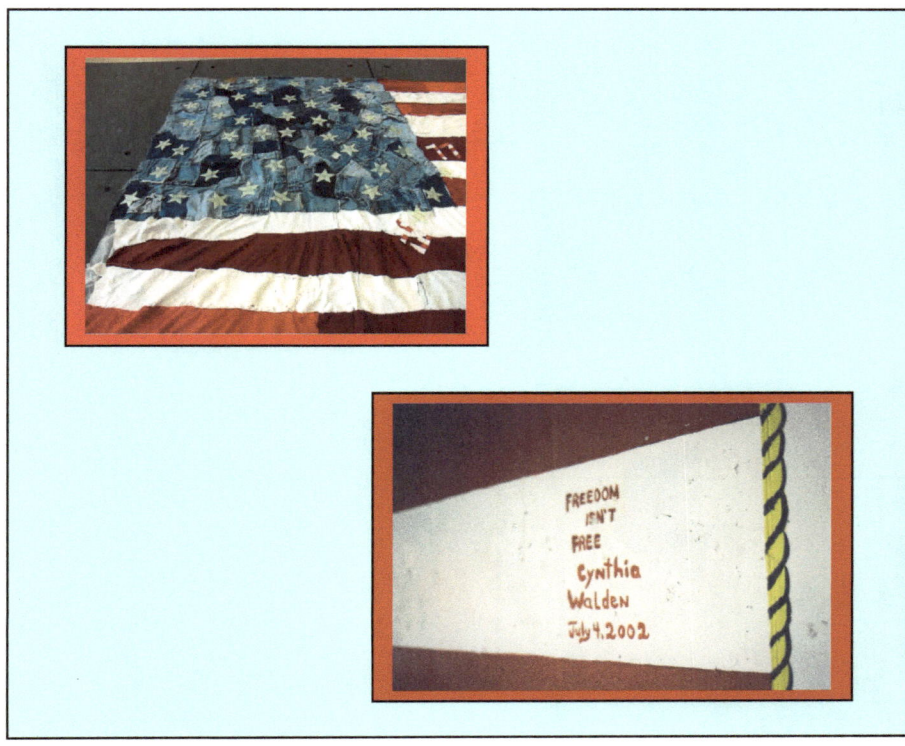

Fig. 4-9 **Signature on USS Indianapolis Mural and 911 tapestry.**
The tapestry honoring 911 was created by Purdue students out of clothing they were wearing on Sept. 11. It is now in the Indiana State Museum on the west wing of the canal past West Street.

Fig. 4-10 **New York Street bridge mural,** West side of bridge
This merry-go-round horse is reminiscent of the Merry-Go Round that was in Broad Ripple Park from the time it was called White City until it was moved to the Children's Museum where it still remains.

Fig. 4-11 **Corn Eater**
New York Street Bridge – West Side
This mural honors corn, an Indiana icon and a popular item at the Indiana State Fair held in August in Indianapolis.

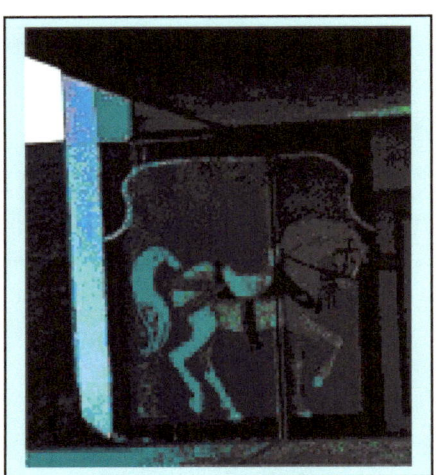

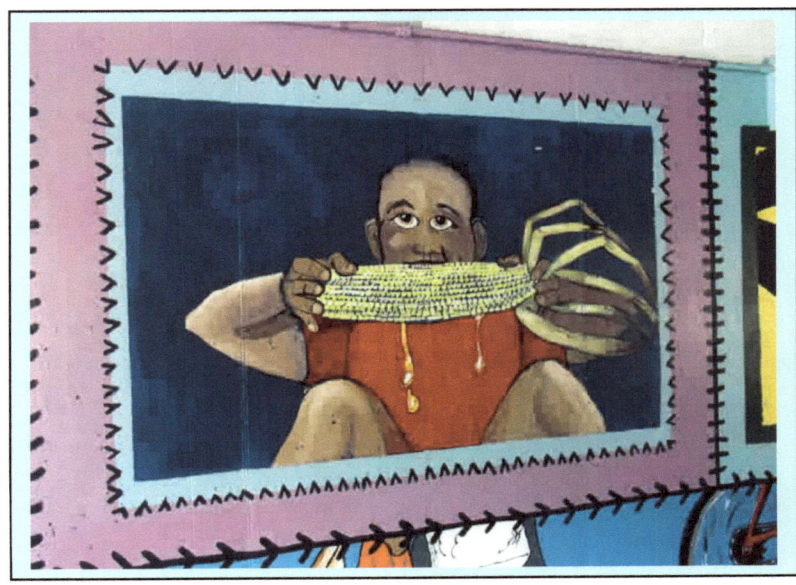

Fig. 4-12 **Covered bridge and checkered flag**, other Indiana icons. New York Street Bridge – West side

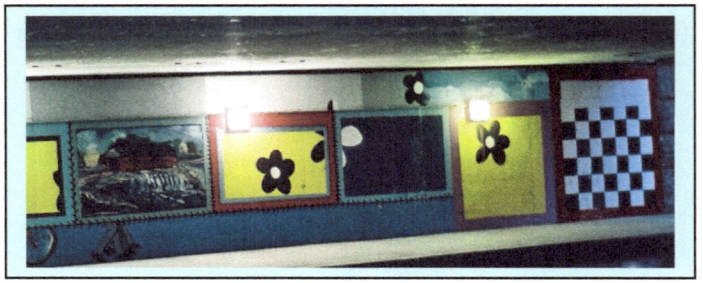

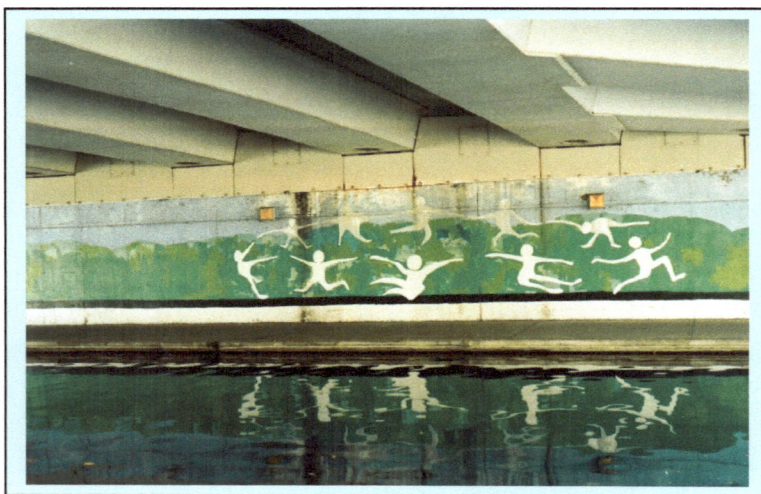

Fig. 4-13 **Dancers Mural** under the Indiana Street bridge reminiscent of Matisse's style.

Fig. 4-14 **Indianapolis Zoo**
Artist: Dan Mitchell went to Butler Univ. and Herron in the 1970s. He studied Portrait Painting and figure drawing and Art Education. He became interested in murals when he worked in a sign painting shop. He was approached by Tuchman Cleaners to paint murals in their stores. The zoo technique uses projection of clip art. Dan feels that grants and official agenda have contributed to the growth of Mural Art in Indy, and art schools have encouraged it.

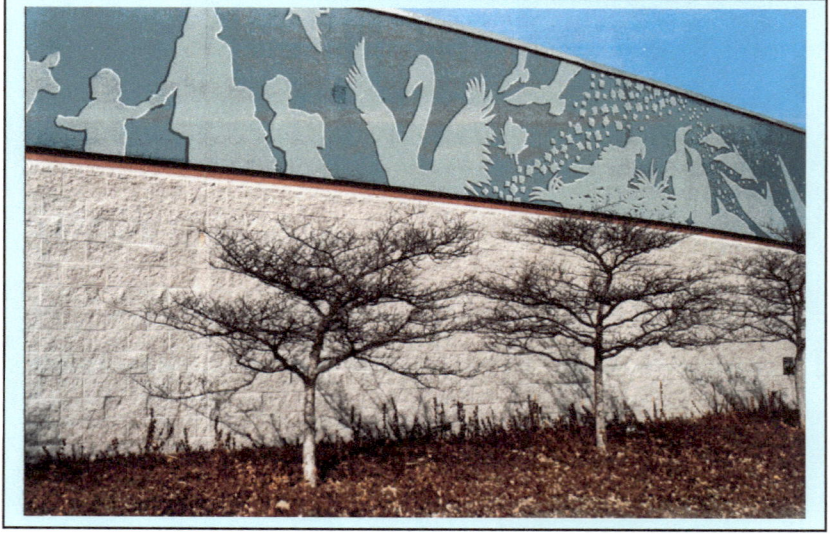

Fig. 4-15 **Bud Schaefer Rotunda**
Artist Andrew Reid

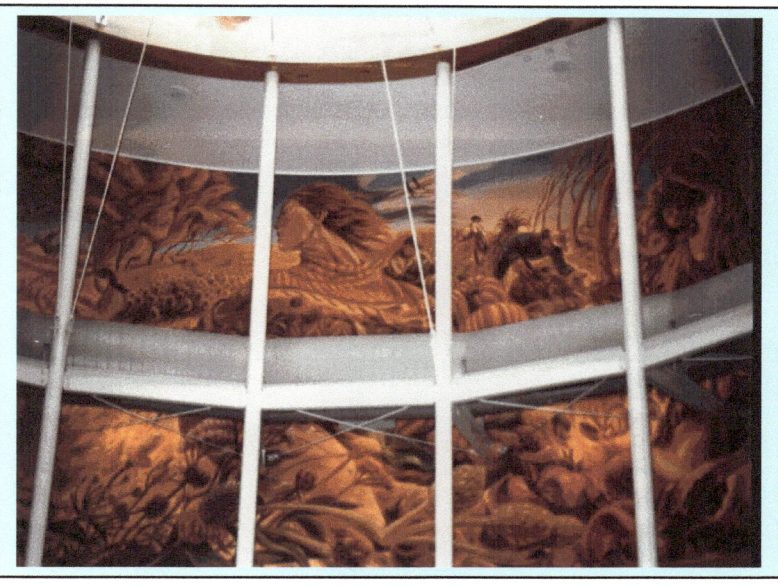

*The first thing to assail your senses is the powerful **mural**. Commissioned from artist **Andrew Reid** following his selection from a national/international design competition, the gripping 360-degree mural tells the story of a wonderful **Midwestern Panorama** gardening experience. The stunning and colorful two-part mural encircles the upper two thirds of the Rotunda, encompassing a sprawling 3,000 square-feet of the mounted painted canvas."* from "Art in White River Gardens" flyer [15]

More on Andrew Reid: No canvas is too large for New Zealand-born muralist Andrew Reid. The 3,000 square foot mural greets hundreds of visitors as they pass through the Garden's silo-shaped entrance and into the adjoining building complex and glass conservatory. The sweeping landscape, entitled Midwestern Panorama, depicts Indiana's distinct seasons and lush, rolling countryside: the tulips and daffodils of spring, the prairie flowers of summer, the brilliant crimson-and-gold foliage of fall. Even winter, with its snow capped evergreens. Reid's mural was chosen from among 100 competing artists and sculptors from U.S., Europe and South America. In preparation for this project, he researched the wildlife, plants and trees of Indiana for months beforehand. [15a]

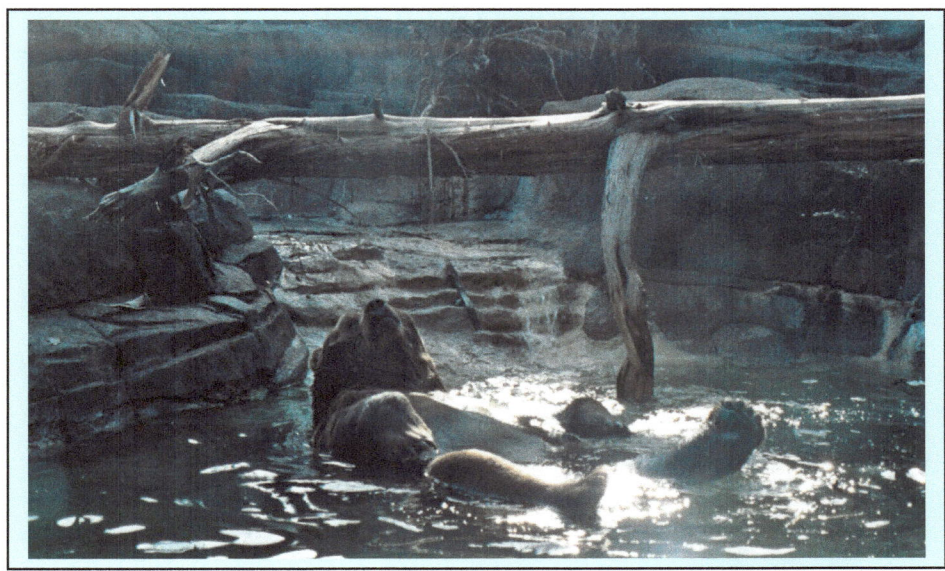

Fig. 4-16 **Bear at Indianapolis Zoo**.

Canal Zoo Gardens Photo List and Sources

1. Intro Indiana Historical Society
   [1] http://www.in.gov/whiteriver/about/canal.html
2. View of Canal Indiana Historical Society and Internet
   [2a] **Title** Indianapolis Canal; **Copyright Notice**Digital image © 2004 Indiana; Historical Society. All
   Item ID P0130_P_BOX20_FOLDER3_UNNUMBERED
   Description View of a nearly dry canal. Trees line one side and railroad tracks the other.
   Creator   W. H. Bass Photo Company
3. Latinos at the Crossroads - Ton Ortega, West Street Bridge, 2002
   [3] September 28, 2002 Indianapolis Star Jennifer Wagner
4. Goddess Mural - Canal near waterfall and Ohio Street Bridge
5. Goddess Mural Barbara Stahl and Girls Inc. etc., 2004
   [4, 5] http://www.kibi.org/gallery_pics/2004_mural/
6. Indiana Scenes, Patricia Wildhack, Ohio Street Bridge, 1999
7. Same
8. USS Indianapolis and Flag Mural, Cynthia Walden, New York Street Bridge, 2002
9. Cynthia Walden's signature on USS Indianapolis mural and Purdue students clothing flag.
10. Merry-Go-Round Horse - west side of New York Street Bridge
11. Corn eater - west side of New York Street Bridge
12. Covered Bridge and checkered flag and black flowers - same
13. Matisse style dancers under Indiana Street Bridge
14. Indianapolis Zoo - Dan Mitchell
15. Bud Schaeffer Rotunda - Andrew Reid
    [15] *from "Art in White River Gardens"* flyer
    [15a] Indpls. Star, Ruth Mullen, June 5, 1999
16. (Bear at the Indianapolis Zoo)

BROAD RIPPLE DISTRICT

Broad Ripple is located on the northeast side of Indianapolis and bounded by the White River, Keystone Avenue, Kessler Boulevard, and Meridian Street. Since its founding as a village in the early 19th century, canals and railroads, streetcars and interurbans, and finally the automobile have influenced the development of the community. Each form of transportation contributed unique elements to the emergence of this settlement, both as a separate village and later as part of the modern city of Indianapolis, thereby providing an interesting study in how transportation can shape and influence community development over time.

The history of this small community along the White River conceivably can be traced to 1816, when Indiana achieved statehood. The state commissioners selected the new site for the state capital because of the White River and the great potential for connecting central Indiana to outside markets. The White River, which meandered through the county, was shallow in spots. [1]

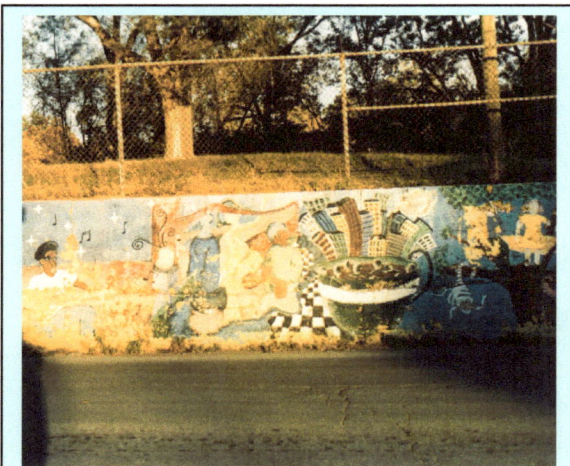

Fig. 5-2 **Jazzy Mural** Broad Ripple H.S. students may have helped. On Westfield Blvd. north of Broad Ripple Ave.

One such location was near the land acquired by McKay and Calip. Here, the land was very wide and broad and the river, when low, "rippled" over the stones in the riverbed. Because it was easy to determine the water's depth at this point, the ripples became a popular river crossing

On June 27, 1839 local residents celebrated the opening of the canal, but their revelry was short-lived. The State of Indiana went bankrupt due to excessive expenses associated with the many internal improvement projects and bad investments by the state. This halted all construction on the canal, leaving slightly more than eight miles of the canal completed between the villages of Broad Ripple and Wellington and the capital city of Indianapolis to the south. Although this effectively ended any hopes for a canal connector for central Indiana, the existing section of the canal linked the northern part of the county with the capital. In July 1839 Robert Earl advertised canal boat service between Indianapolis and Broad Ripple. In 1884, the U.S. Post Office Department located the office in Wellington but retained the name Broad Ripple. As a result of this action, the two rival communities merged and incorporated as Broad Ripple with some 150 residents.

In the early 1900s, Indianapolis residents, aided by the availability of the streetcar lines, began coming to the Broad Ripple area as a summer retreat from the city. The Indianapolis Star in July 1911 described the many residents who had built summer homes-ranging from rustic cottages to comfortable homes with electricity and indoor plumbing-and the numerous recreational activities of summer visitors along the banks of White River. By this time, some families had become year-round residents and used the streetcars or their own automobiles to commute to downtown Indianapolis workplaces. [2]

Besides the summer cottages, Broad Ripple supported many recreational opportunities, which attracted day visitors. Boat clubs and steamships offered opportunities to enjoy the river. The small steamship "Sunshine" arrived in Broad Ripple and plied its way along White River in 1897. Other small ships offered music, dancing, and one-day trips on the river. Some encountered serious problems navigating the river, running aground in shallow spots, being damaged by ice, or-as in one peculiar case-sinking because the passengers all ran to one side of the boat to view a pretty girl.

The high point of Broad Ripple's recreational development, however, was the opening of White City Amusement Park on May 26,1906. The park occupied land previously owned by the Huffman and subsequently Dawson families. It had served as a popular picnic spot, until building contractors Morton and Stanton bought the land and constructed the amusement park. In 1907 W. H. Tabb and Robert C. Light formed the White City Company of Indianapolis and obtained a nine-year operating lease for the facility. The park offered a variety of mechanical rides and amusements, which rivaled those in New York's Coney Island or Chicago's 1893 Columbian Exposition (from which Broad Ripple's amusement park took its name "White City"). White City provided not only a destination for visitors but also a source of employment for local residents. The streetcars and inter-urbans ran regular schedules between Broad Ripple and Indianapolis, primarily along College Avenue. The turn-around for the College line, completed in 1894, was located at the park's front gate, which contributed to the growth and popularity of the site. Over the next two years, the park's operators introduced new rides and attractions, completed a concrete-lined bathing beach along the river, and constructed a four-acre swimming pool, touted as "the largest affair of the kind in the country." On June 26, 1908, the day before the pool was scheduled to open, White City Amusement Park burned to the ground. Owners estimated losses at $160,000, none of which was covered by insurance. [3]

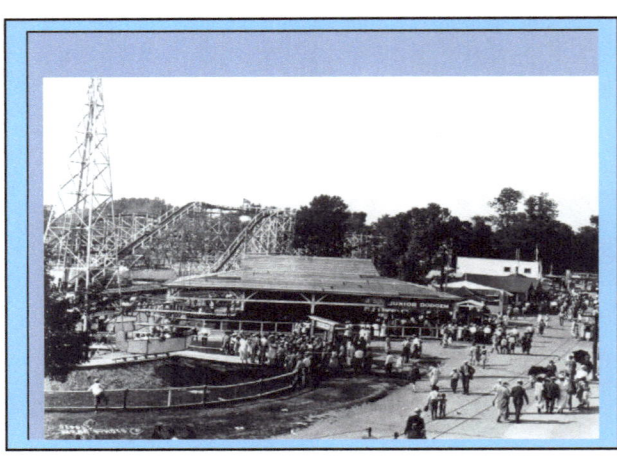

Fig. 5-3 **Broad Ripple Park (White City)**

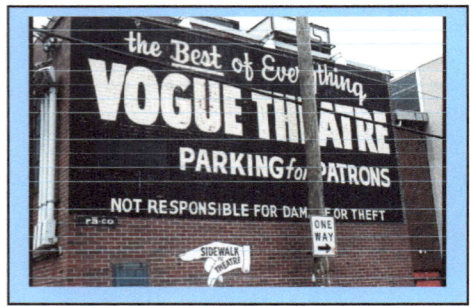

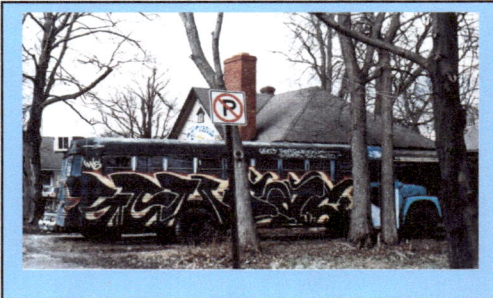

Fig. 5-4 **Vogue Theater Sign and Bus in Broad Ripple**
Between the years 1922 and 1959 Broad Ripple came into its own as a community. The arrival of Indianapolis city services such as police and fire (the first fire station was completed in 1922) encouraged residential development. The commercial areas and the residential districts also witnessed growth. Broad Ripple's schools became part of the Indianapolis Public Schools system in 1923. A storefront branch of the Indianapolis Public Library opened in 1930, which, because of continued community growth, was replaced in 1949 with the first public library branch to be constructed in the county since 1914. The Vogue Theater opened as a first-run movie house in June 1938. A new post office opened in 1940. Stores located in downtown Indianapolis began establishing branches in Broad Ripple; the William H. Block Company opened a store in 1954, and clothing retailer L. Strauss followed in 1956. Kroger's and Standard grocery stores also opened. City directories of the period showed 100 businesses present in 1930 and 252 in 1951. [4]

Fig. 5-5 **Old Flag mural in alley behind Vogue Theater**

Since the 1970s, the community has experienced what is commonly referred to as the "Broad Ripple Revival."

During this period, low commercial rent stimulated the opening of small specialty stores and nightclubs, giving Broad Ripple an atmosphere distinct from any other part of Indianapolis. Teenagers and young adults began to frequent the nightspots. The Vogue, which re-opened in 1980 as a nightclub highlighting both local and national artists, spurred additional commercial development. Broad Ripple residents recently participated in the opening of the new Monon Trail, a "rail-to-trail" project along the old Monon railroad line, originating at the canal and Broad Ripple Avenue and extending north to 86th Street in Nora. [5]

Note: The trail now extends from Carmel to downtown.

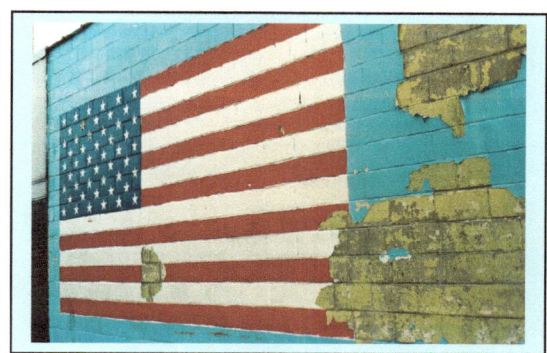

Fig. 5-6 **Grafitti Expo Mural** Alley behind Broad Ripple Post Office, 6255 Carrolton Ave.

Concrete canvas gives artists creative outlet. Young allowed to express themselves, while community gets a little sprucing up. Members of the Broad Ripple community created a Labor Day art festival that allowed graffiti artists to express themselves in a way that didn't deface property. More than 40 artists created works. -- Rich Miller / staff photo. (written by Beth Douglas Silcox)

Graffiti -- art or misdemeanor? That's what the Broad Ripple Village Association had been asking before Matthew Lawrence and the Indianapolis Art Center stepped in to provide a definitive answer.

"Tagging" property with graffiti was a big problem in Broad Ripple. Aerosol crews took to the streets in initiation-type raids, painting parking meters, walls and anything else that stood still. Until, that is, Broad Ripple made room for the unique art form. Graffiti causes property damage and is a misdemeanor, so the Broad Ripple Village Association hooked up with the

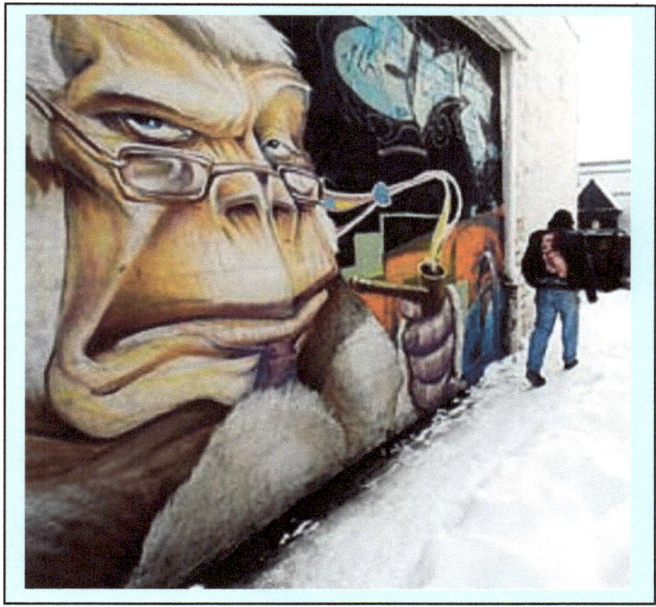

Indianapolis Police Department and formed a Graffiti Task Force, which set about recording, reporting and removing graffiti. "When some kids were caught, we went to juvenile court and had all these pictures. We showed them to the judge," said Elaine Zuckerman of the Broad Ripple Village Association.

Punishment came in the form of community service -- 250 hours each. The aerosol artists cleaned up the trash left behind by Friday crowds in the village and removed graffiti. "In working with these kids and seeing what they were doing," Zuckerman said, "I saw some of them are really artists. They're just kids, and they don't want to put their art on a canvas . . . and be that inhibited, so the Graffiti Task Force worked itself into doing a graffiti jam." In other words, they came up with a Labor Day event that let graffiti artists do their thing legitimately. [6]

Officially named "Subsurface 500," the graffiti event was a collaborative effort among the art center, Broad Ripple Village Association and the Trans-global Urban Art Project.

Matthew Lawrence is the 24-year-old aerosol artist who heads up the Trans-global Urban Art Project. His group recruits artists to paint legal aerosol murals and works to dispel the common belief that all graffiti tagging is gang-related.

Simply put, a graffiti crew paints. Sometimes they collaborate on mural-sized productions, while other times individuals will disperse for a graffiti raid through a neighborhood. While graffiti is illegal under property damage laws, it takes great skill to create the art some buildings wear. "It's like using an air brush, only on a larger scale," Lawrence said. "There are different techniques involved with aerosol art that are a lot easier to obtain with aerosol than with brushes."

Egyptian eyes and streaming sunbeams gaze over a field of pyramids in shades of blue, yellow and green, while ghostly figures repair gear works inside a darkened machine farther down the mural. T-boning into the alley is another mural wall running along the access drive to the U.S. Post Office loading docks. Here, a white-haired man with a spyglass in hand and black swan on his back, keeps watch over the mural. This kindly gentleman will likely disappear, as Subsurface 500 artists remake the mural in the second annual Labor Day weekend event. [7]

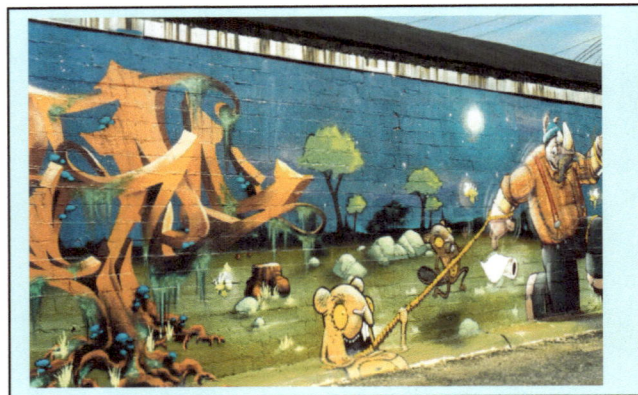 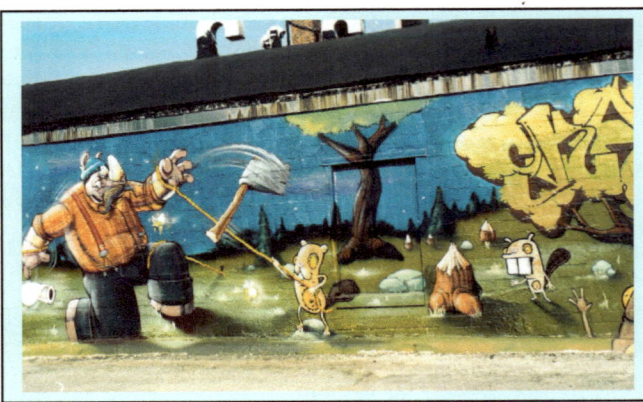

Fig. 5-7 **Subsurface 2004 Mural** Artist D. Ross, Broad Ripple Environmental Theme

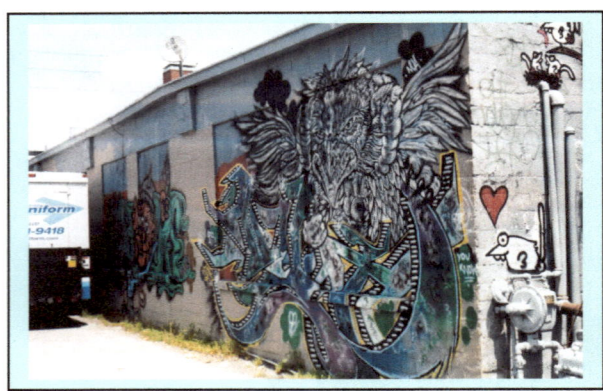

Fig. 5-8 **Subsurface 2004 Event mural.**
The Midwest graffiti expo was first held in 2002. Lawrence said he is trying to make it an annual event so the artists can work with a community that might be traditionally opposed to graffiti and to create a positive alternative to defacing property. Lawrence said the public's perception of graffiti art might be influenced by its limited knowledge of the topic but added that the first expo was received well and has helped build a relationship between the city and the artists in the past. [8] "There's a very positive atmosphere when (the artists) come up," Lawrence said. "It's a chance for a public to get to know the artist when they come to perform their work, and it put the artists out there for the public to see."

Fig. 5-9 **Subsurface 2004 Event mural**
Local Broad Ripple businesses, such as Alley Cat Lounge and Passwater Auto Specialists, have volunteered wall space for the event. "I think (the mural) turned out well last time," said Tim Oprisui, owner of Old Pro's Table, which is volunteering wall space for the expo. Oprisui also said the art expo has had two positive influences for the Broad Ripple neighborhood. "It has decreased graffiti and vandalism in the neighborhood and also helps the cultural aspects for the area," he said. "I think people who do graffiti will pick a plain wall, but they won't damage a piece of art. Since the first mural was painted two years ago, there hasn't been any vandalism done to it," Oprisui said. [9]

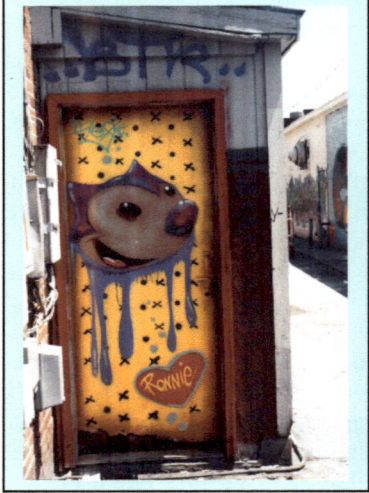 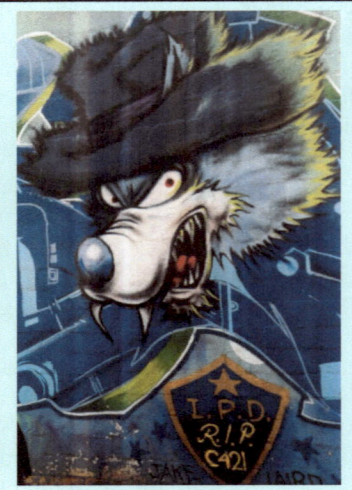

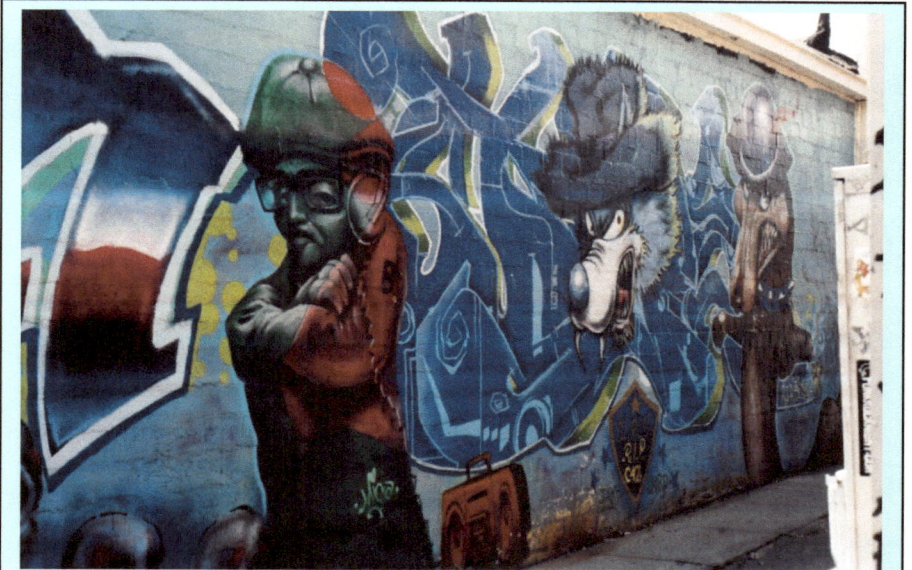

Fig. 5-10 **Subsurface 2004 Event Mural**
Lawrence said the artist selection was by invitation only. The artists come from a wide variety of backgrounds, including professional mural artists, customer sign painters, movie set designers and children's book illustrators. Local disc jockeys and musical groups were added to the line-up and performed from 9 p.m. to 3 a.m. during the expo. Subsurface took place in the Broad Ripple Village Cultural District in the alley east of the Broad Ripple Post Office, located at 6255 Carrollton Ave., which runs between 61st Street and Broad Ripple Avenue. [10]

The event was free and open to the public.

Fig. 5-11-13 **Cupid and Italian Balcony Scenes.**
Massage Therapist Business– 62nd and College
Artist: Sylvia Andrews

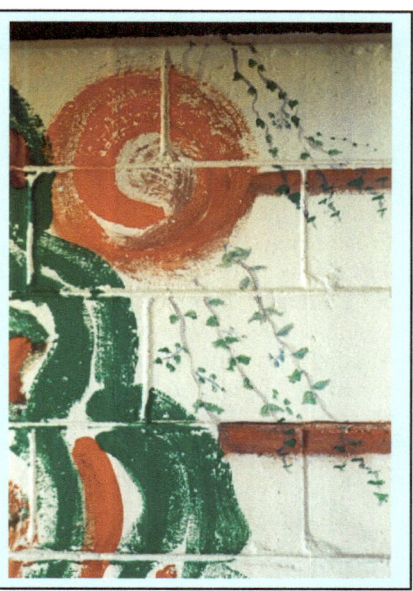

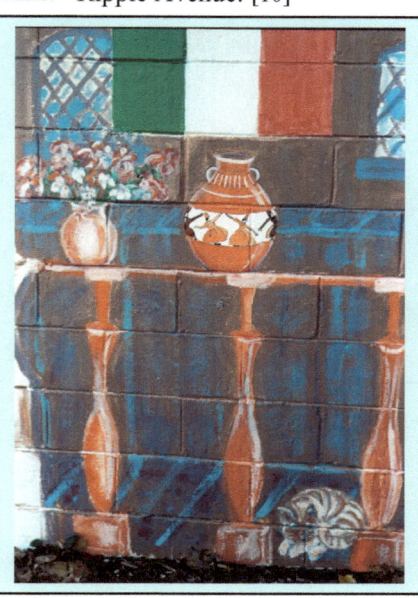

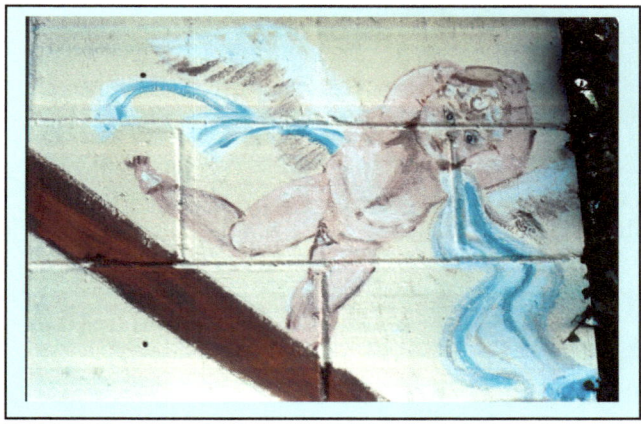

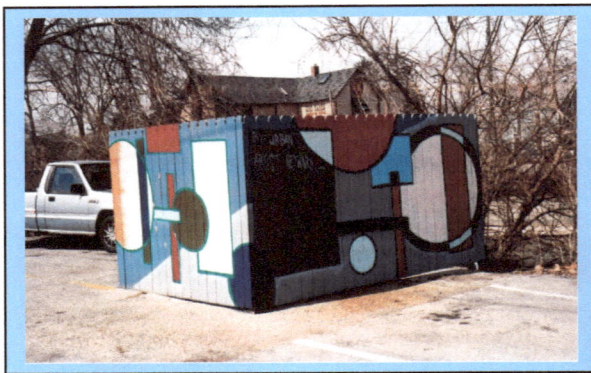

Fig. 5-14 **Trash container fence** on canal behind Monon Coffee Shop (64th Street) By Urban Artist Network

Fig. 5-15 **Broad Ripple Swimming Pool Mural**
Pool is just east of Broad Ripple on 62nd street in Broad Ripple park.

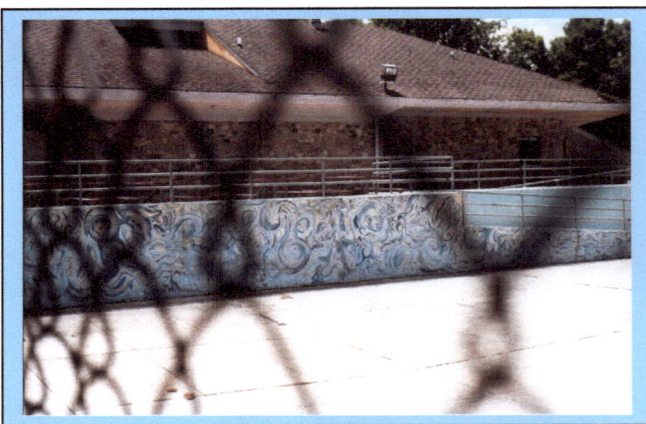

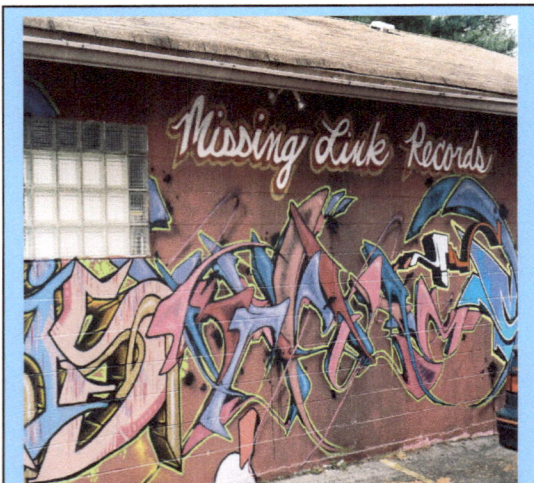

Fig. 5-16 **Missing Link Records** Now at 4905 N. College
Back in the summer of 1993, Missing Link opened its doors in the former location of Ardvark Records at the corner of Shelby and Hanna on the city's south side. The next year, the store relocated to Broad Ripple. Missing Link has long supported independent and local music, though it is best known for its massive selection of new, used and rare vinyl records. From classical to classic rock, Missing Link has a wide selection of records in all genres.
Missing Link's stock has grown well beyond 50,000 pieces; it's now one of the largest vinyl record stores in the Midwest. DJ's and record collectors travel from great distances to dig through the ever-growing stacks of LP's, 45's and 78's.
http://www.missinglinkrecords.com/about.htm

Fig. 5-17 **Rainbow Bridge.** Guilford St. over Canal.

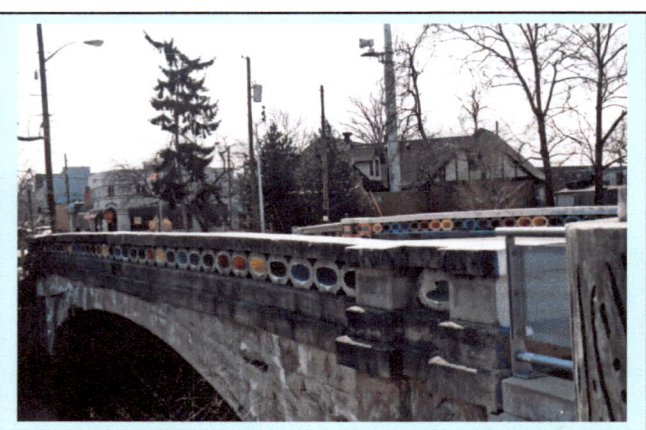

Fig. 5-18 **Biscuits Café** – Monon Trail just south of 62nd
Artists Joshua Wells and Dan Thompson
Paintsubsurface.org

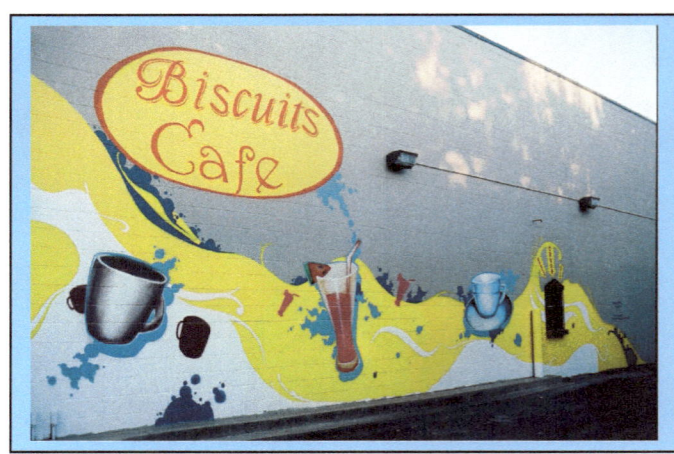

Fig. 5-19 **Protect Pollinators**, Rene's Bakery, Coil Street near the Monon Trail. Artist: Sylvia Andrews (2007)

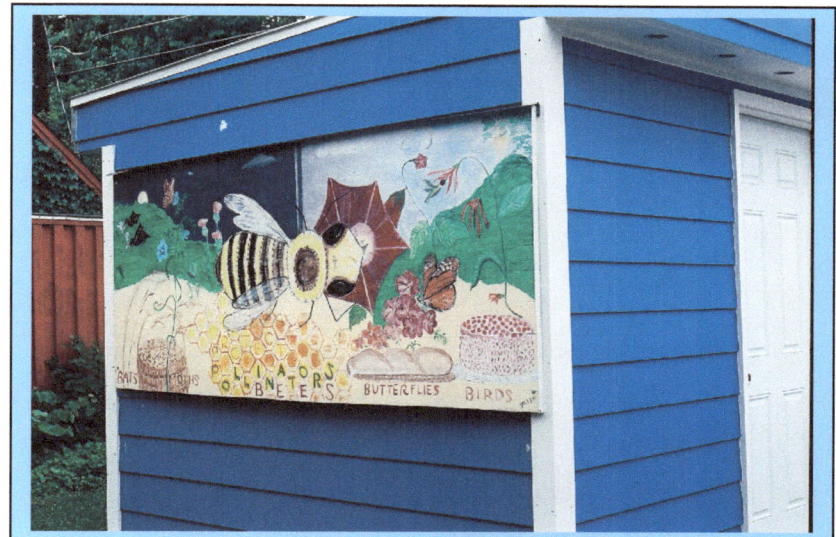

Fig. 5-20 **T-shirt art. (One Tequila, Two Tequila, Three Tequila, Four) etc.** Old Stone Mug, now Steel Pony, North College

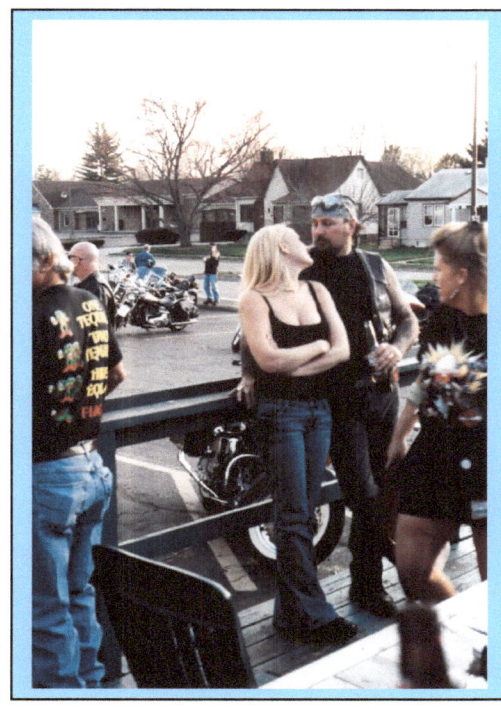

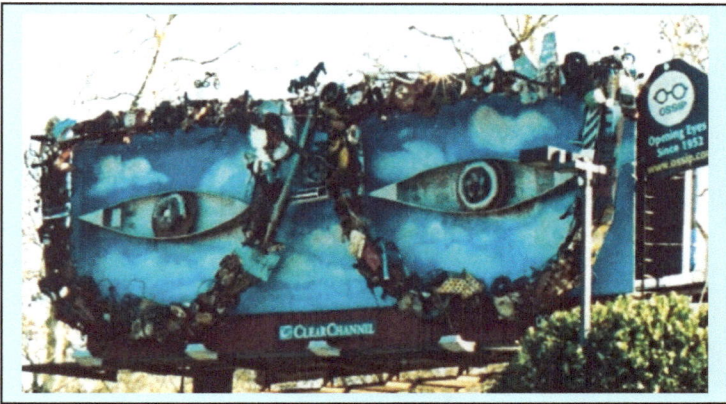

Fig. 5-21 **Dr. Ossip's Eyes**
Dr. Ossip, optometrist, has been in Broad Ripple for decades. This billboard has kept a vigilant watch over Broad Ripple, by day and by night. Dr. Ossip's son now runs the business.
Located on Broad Ripple Ave. by Broad Ripple High School and made of canoes, bicycles, weather vanes, tires etc. (No longer there.)

Fig. 5-22 **Posh Petals** - On 52ⁿᵈ Street near College Ave.

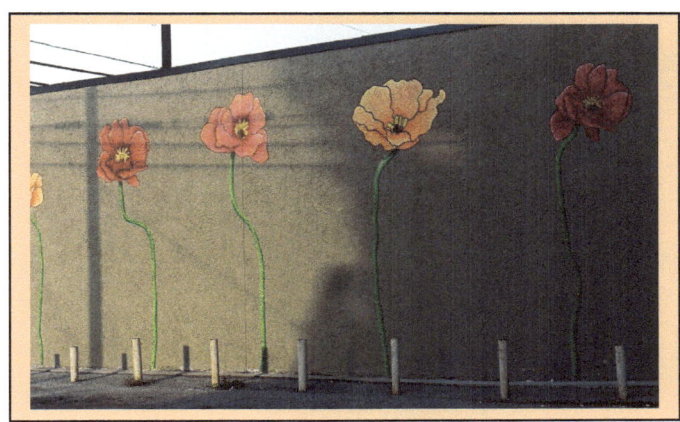

Broad Ripple Village - Photo List and Sources

1. Introduction

   [1] http://www.polis.iupui.edu/RUC/Neighborhoods/BroadRipple/BRNarrative.htm

2. Mural on Westfield Blvd. and 65th

   [2] http://www.polis.iupui.edu/RUC/Neighborhoods/BroadRipple/BRNarrative.htm

3. Image of Broad Ripple Amusement Park (Indiana Historical Society Image Database.

   Title Broad Ripple Amusement Park **Item ID** P0130_P_BOX45_FOLDER5_92861-F **Description** Three amusement park rides are shown: Sea Planes, Junior Dodgem, and the roller coaster. **Creator** W. H. Bass Photo Company **Date** 1925 **Geographic Location** Indiana--Indianapolis **Format of Original** Photographic print, b&w **Size of Original** 8 x 10 in. **Digital Format** JPG **Owning Institution** Indiana Historical Society **Collection Name** W. H. Bass Photo Company Collection **Collection Number** P 0130 **Copyright Notice** Digital image © 2004 Indiana Historical Society. All Rights Reserved. **Full resolution** http://images.indianahistory.org/fullres/P0130/volume0/P0130_P_BOX45_FOLDER5_92861-F.tif

   [3] http://www.polis.iupui.edu/RUC/Neighborhoods/BroadRipple/BRNarrative.htm

4. Bus parked in Broad Ripple and Vogue Theater sign.

   [4]http://www.polis.iupui.edu/RUC/Neighborhoods/BroadRipple/BRNarrative.htm

5. Old Flag Mural in alley behind Vogue Theater

   [5]http://www.polis.iupui.edu/RUC/Neighborhoods/BroadRipple/BRNarrative.htm

6. Graffiti Expo Mural in alley south of Broad Ripple Ave.

   [6]By Beth Douglass Silcox Indianapolis Star March 24, 2003 More than 40 artists created works. - Rich Miller / staff photo

7. 2004 Subsurface Event mural by artist D. Ross, Broad Ripple

   [7] By Beth Douglass Silcox Indianapolis Star March 24, 2003 More than 40 artists created works.

8. Subsurface Event mural

9. Subsurface Event mural

   [8-9] Indiana Daily Student idsnews.com Thursday, September 09,2004
   Canned Art, Indianapolis holds its second graffiti art expositions. By Tony Sams
   http://www.idsnews.com/news/story.php?id+26792

10. Subsurface Event Mural

    [10] Indiana Daily Student idsnews.com Thursday, September 09,2004 (same as above)

11-13. Massage Therapy Mural reflecting Italian themes - Sylvia Andrews 62nd and College

14. Trash Area behind Monon Coffee Shop on Canal

15. Broad Ripple Swimming Pool, Broad Ripple Avenue

16. Missing Links Record Store, College Avenue

17. Rainbow Bridge, Guilford over canal.

18. Biscuits Café, Broad Ripple Ave. and Monon Trail - Joshua Wells, Dan Thompson

19. Rene's Bakery, Coil Street near the Monon Trail - Sylvia Andrews - Protect Pollinators

20. Some T-Shirt Art - Old Stone Mug, now Steel Pony

21. Dr. Ossip billboard, Broad Ripple Ave. Across from Broad Ripple High School

22. Posh Petals - On 52nd Street just west of College

The Monon railroad track ran into Indianapolis from the north side through Carmel and Nora and parallel to College Avenue as it approached downtown. The following paragraph talks about the Monon Trail which has replaced the track. The Rails to Trails organization was also instrumental in the history of the trail.

Ray Irvin: A Man on a Mission by Michael J. Nolan (www.indianapoliseye.com)
Indianapolis has always been fortunate to have many visionary leaders whose ideas and energy have made it a better place. Ray's legacy as director of the Indianapolis Greenways is miles and miles of trails weaving their way throughout the city and weaving the city back together. The trail has also increased neighborhood housing values, encouraged the growth of native species and kept historical railroad paraphernalia alive.

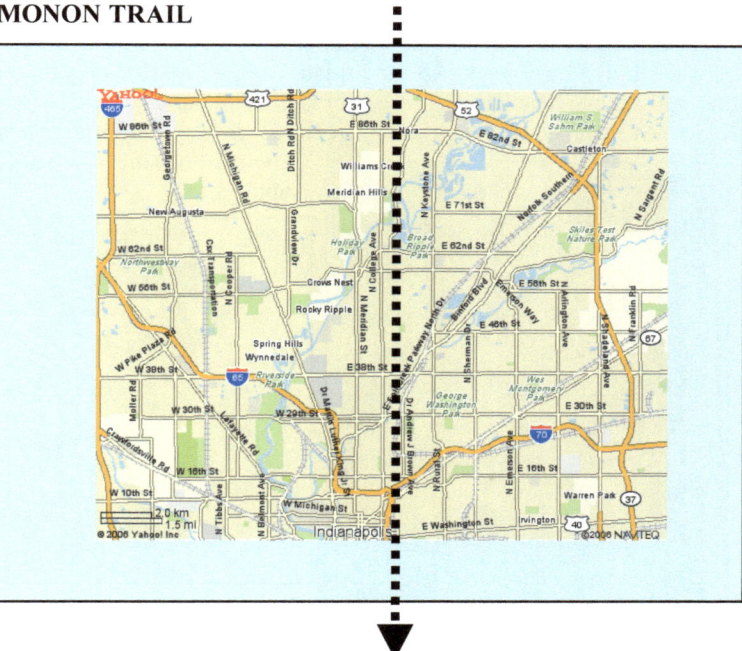

Ray Irvin left his post as Indy Greenways administrator to become director of Bikeways for the state Department of Transportation at the beginning of 2006. He envisioned the greenways as more than all the above however. He envisioned them as a means of attracting people who can transform a rustbelt city to a biotech city, a vehicle for fighting obesity and boredom and a way to develop a sense of community. They have actually been all this as well as a wonderful forum for artists of all kinds, especially muralists. [1]

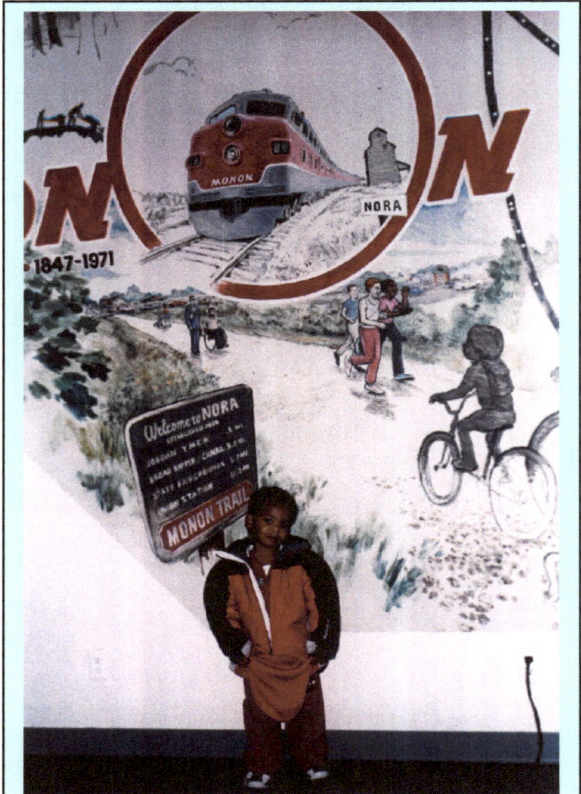

Fig. 6-2 **Monon Trail Mural** - Tuchman Cleaners 1470 E. 86th
Artist: Dan Mitchell
Dan attended Butler University and Herron School of Art in the 70's. He studied portrait painting and figure drawing and art education. He became interested in murals when he worked in a sign painting shop.
Dan was approached by Tuchman Cleaners to paint murals in their stores. He chose themes related to the history of the neighborhoods in which the stores were located. This mural shows a realistic illustration style. It is a community oriented type mural which connects the store with its surroundings. It is also historical and geographical and promotes the Monon Trail. [2]

Fig. 6-3 **Arthur Jordan YMCA Mural**

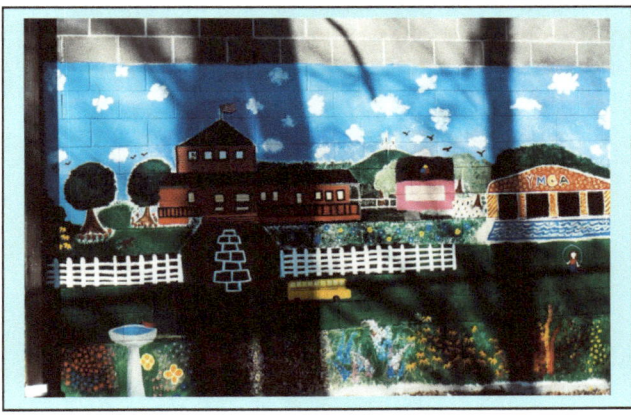

Artist Linda Loman painted this mural at a Monon Trail access point just south of 86th street in Nora. -- A partnership between Indy Greenways, Arthur Jordan YMCA, ACE Hardware, and Butler, Fairman & Seufert continues to improve this trail access. The access has been resurfaced and continually treated for weeds and invasive species. Butler Fairman & Seufert installed a memorial bench for green-way enthusiast Nelson Steele. The YMCA recruited mural artist Linda Lowman to paint the wall of ACE's building, and ACE donated all necessary supplies.

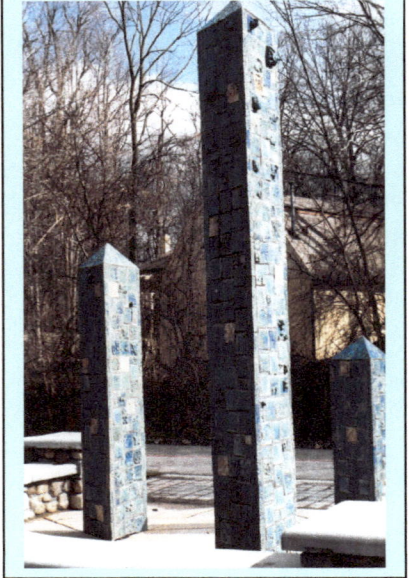

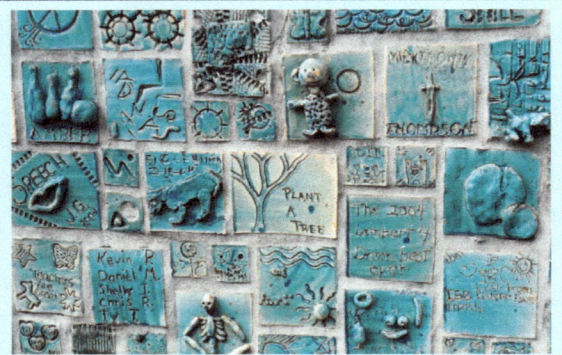

Fig. 6-4 Indiana **School for the Blind** Monon Trailhead Mosaics. Artist: Tim Ryan - Indianapolis, Indiana (north of 79th street).

The focal point of the plaza, both visually and audibly, is a new sculptural fountain piece designed specifically for the site. Tim Ryan, a local visually-impaired artist designed a series of three pillars as the fountain's central piece. The pillar facades serve to support several individual ceramic tile art pieces designed by the students at the school for the Blind. The campus of the Indiana School for the Blind sits adjacent to the Monon Trail.

The campus was separated from the corridor as a safety issue during the railroad days, but the design of the corridor as a pedestrian trail system brings new possibilities to the project. The Monon Trail has been one of the most successful community projects in this area of Indianapolis and has had a huge impact on the community. After several meetings with school officials, the connection between the campus and the trail was selected as a high priority need. Students routinely are given day passes to leave campus to walk to Broad Ripple (several blocks south).

Fig. 6-5 **Sculptured Mural**
Sculptured mural near the Whistle Stop and 65th street. The whistle Stop used to be the old railroad station in Broad Ripple.

Previously, when students left the campus they were forced to use walks along the very busy College Avenue. Although students learned from the experience of being interjected into typical traffic patterns, the walks and streets were not adequately designed for use, and in some cases there were not even sidewalks. The trail offers a direct pedestrian linkage between the campus and Broad Ripple with relatively few street crossings. In addition, the route connects the campus to a nature preserve as well as the White River. [5]

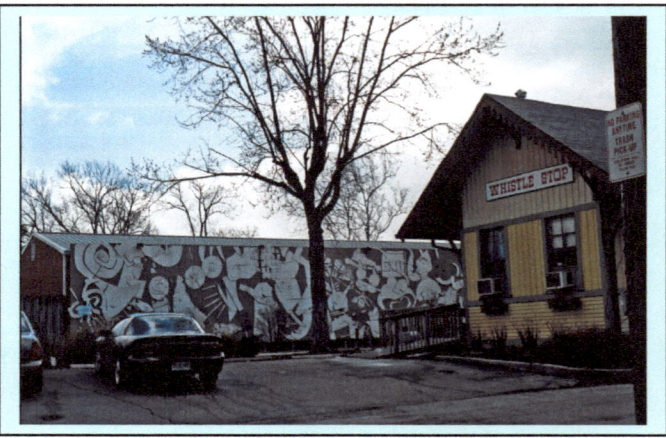

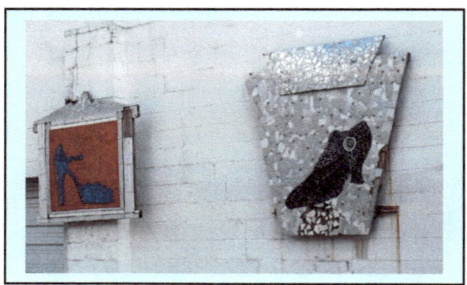

Fig. 6-6 **Shoes** near 65th and Monon Trail

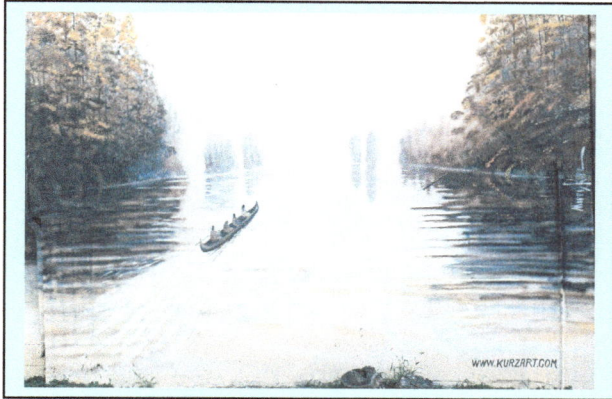

Fig. 6-7 **River Mural**
Artist: Morris Kurz, 64th Street Mural

Morris is a mural artist who presented his rendering to the Greenways committee in 2005. Mr. Kurz took it upon himself to supply the materials to repair the building. Greenways supplied the paint, but Mr. Kurz donated his work, time and other material for preparing the building for his art.

When the mural was vandalized by graffiti soon after it was painted, Kurz took it in stride and repainted the mural, taking the opportunity to make some improvements.

The murals on the trail are now graffiti coated. [7]

Fig. 6-8, 9 **The Monon Trail Urban Art Wall Project The Nature of Indy.** Indy Parks Greenways along with their neighbors along the Monon Trail – Urban Arts Wall Project. Many schools were involved.

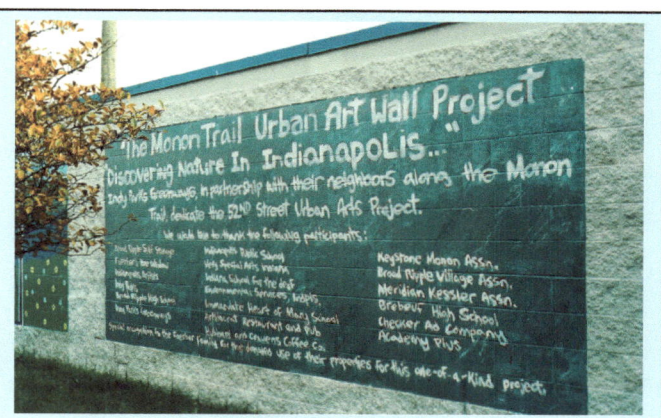

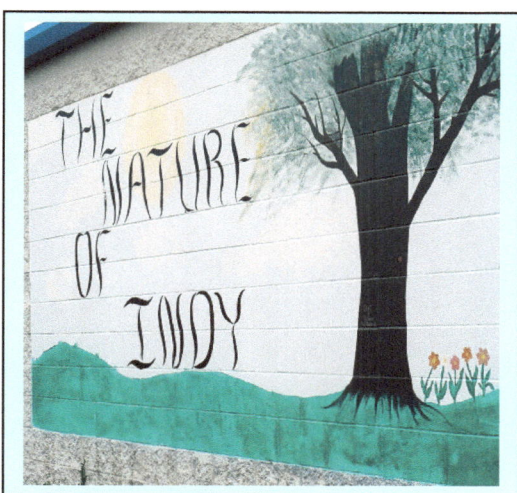

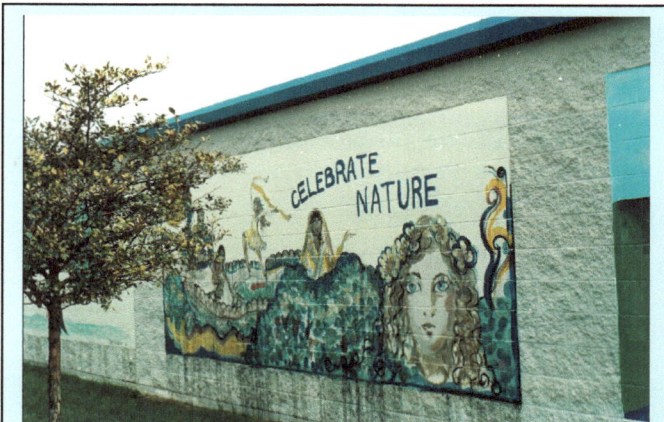

Fig. 6-10 **Celebrate Nature**

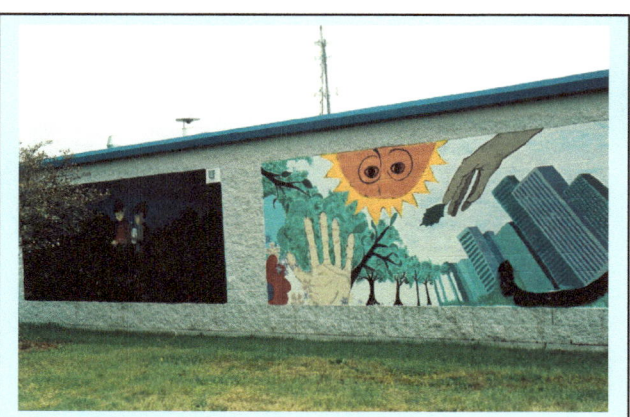

Fig. 6-11 **Hello Sunshine**

Fig. 6-12

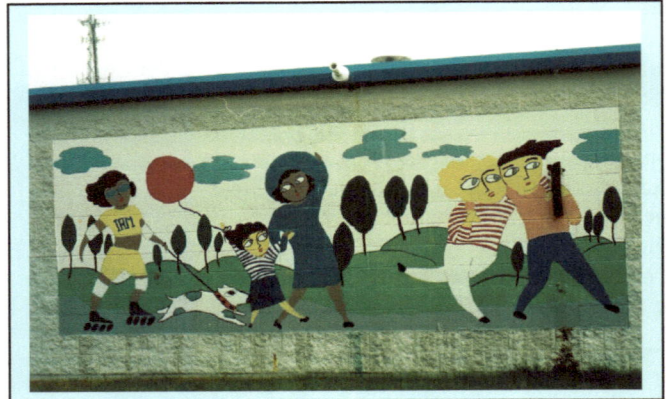

Fig 6-13

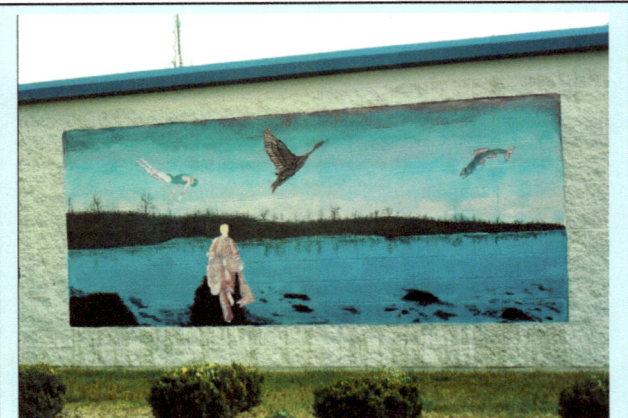

Fig. 6-14

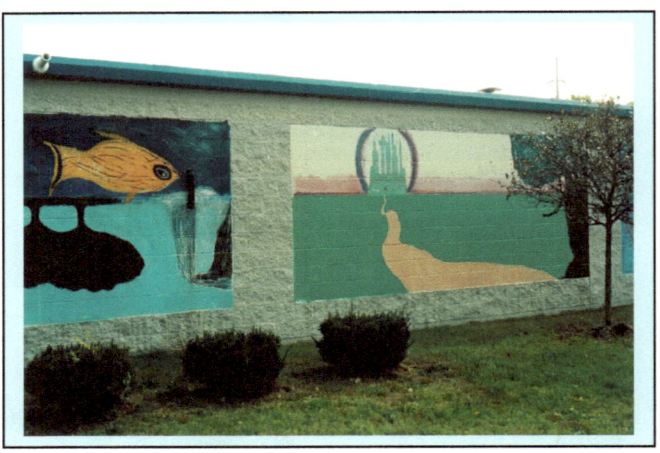

Fig 6-15

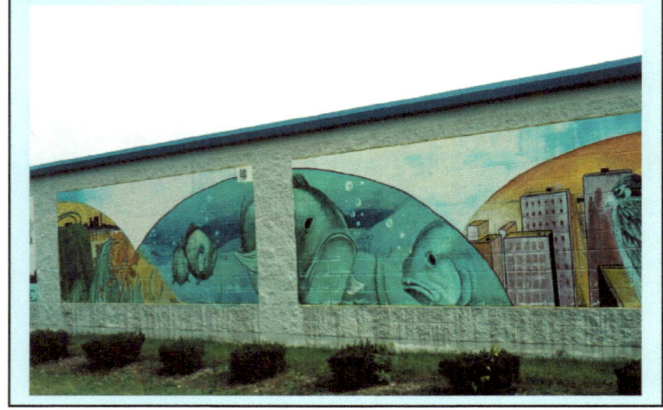

Fig 6-16

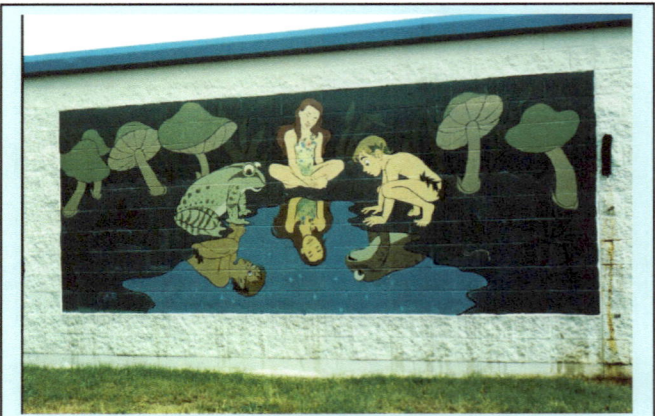

Fig. 6-17 This mural says, "We have One Earth"
Note the flag, eagle and tank symbolism.

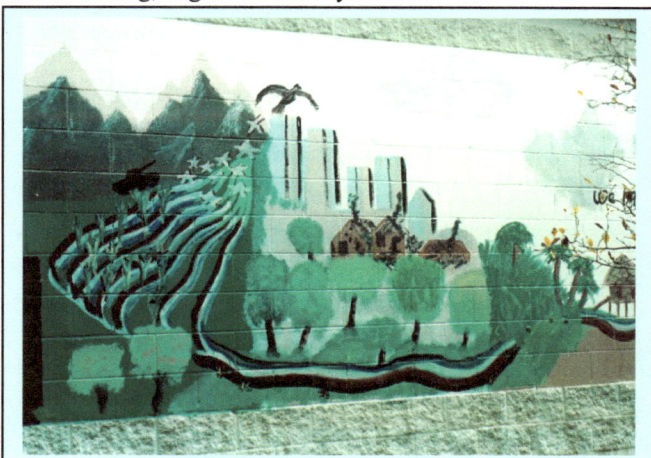

6-18 The mural looks like a quilt pattern.

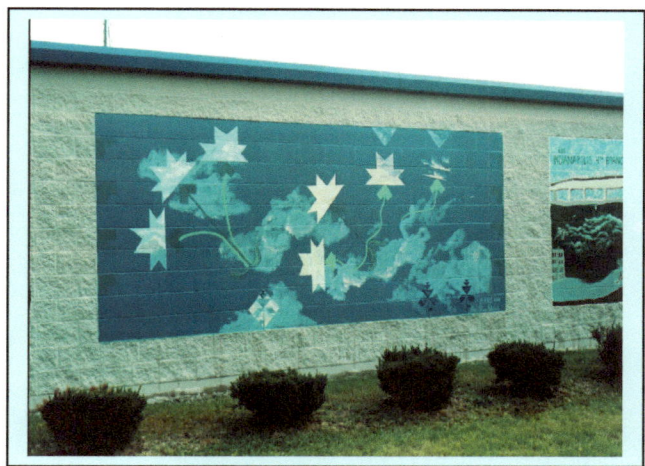

Fig. 6-19

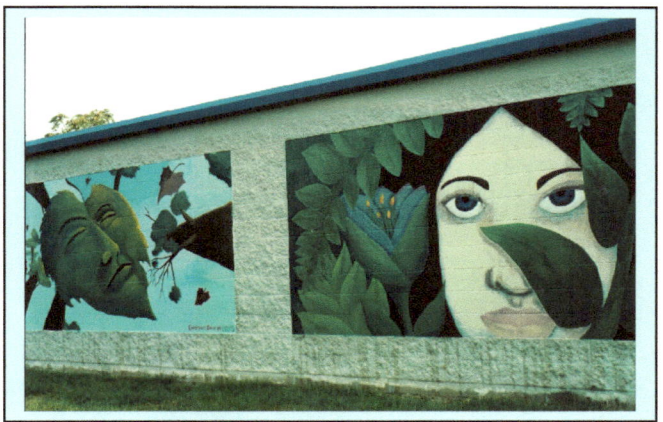

Fig. 6-20

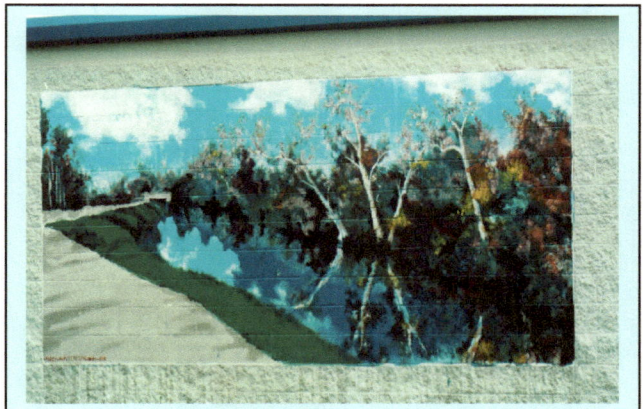

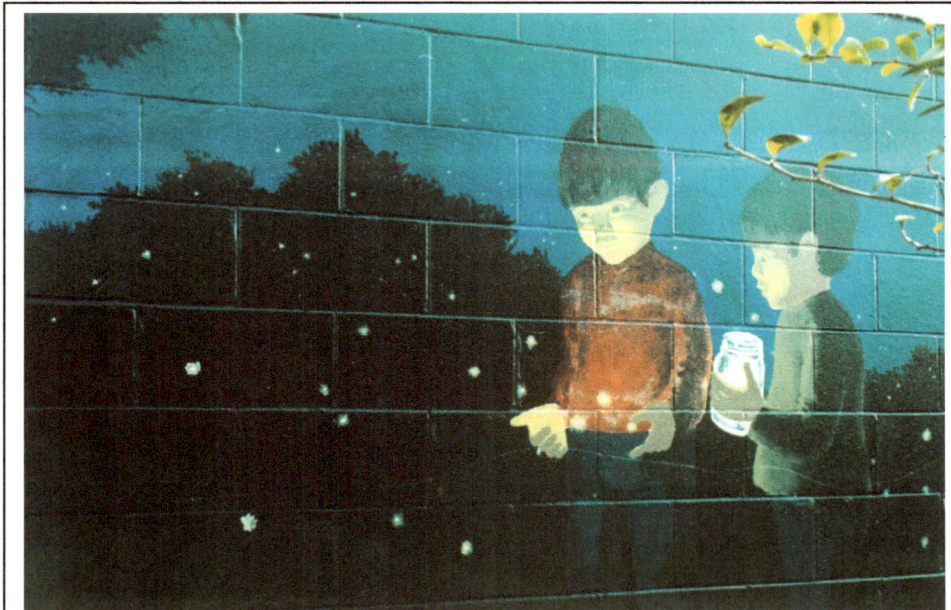

Fig 6-21 **Fireflies**

49

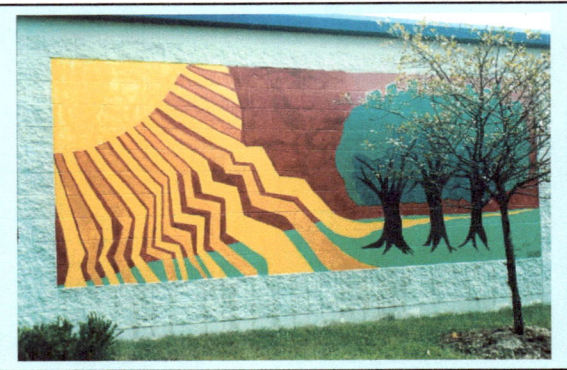

Fig. 6-22-25 More murals in Nature of Indy project.   (And there are more there to see.)

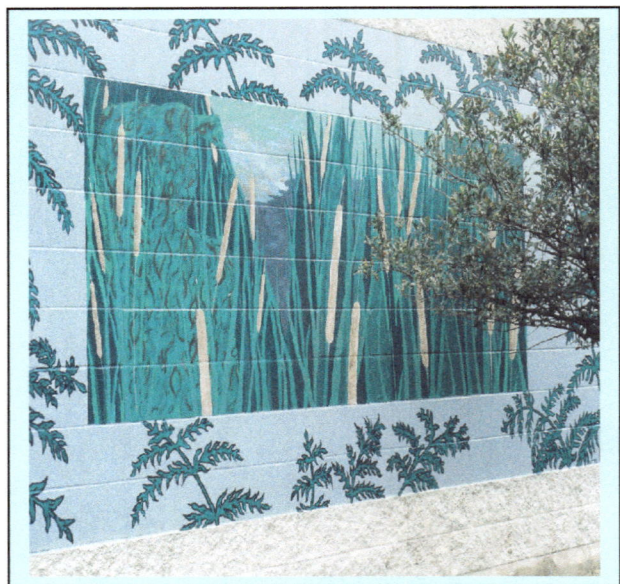

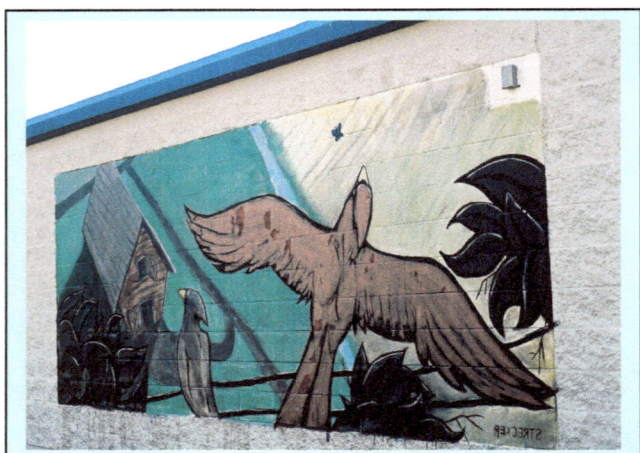

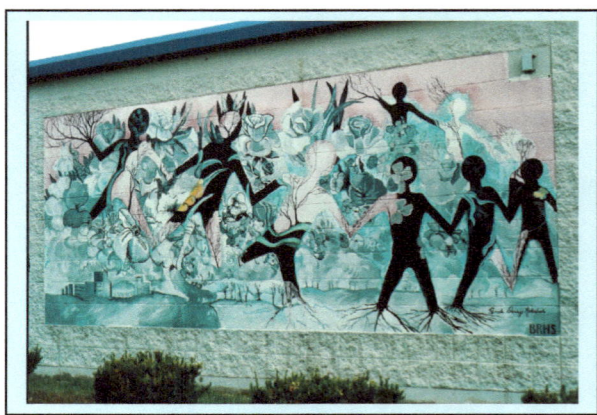

Fig. 6-26 **Wall of Fame** The first generation of graffiti writers plied their trade on the walls of "The Drake," an abandoned building near 52nd Street that butts up against the railroad tracks that have now become the Monon Trail. On the other side of the tracks, the back wall of the Indiana Carpet Distributor's was known as the "Wall of Fame," where only the city's best and most privileged writers would dare to paint.

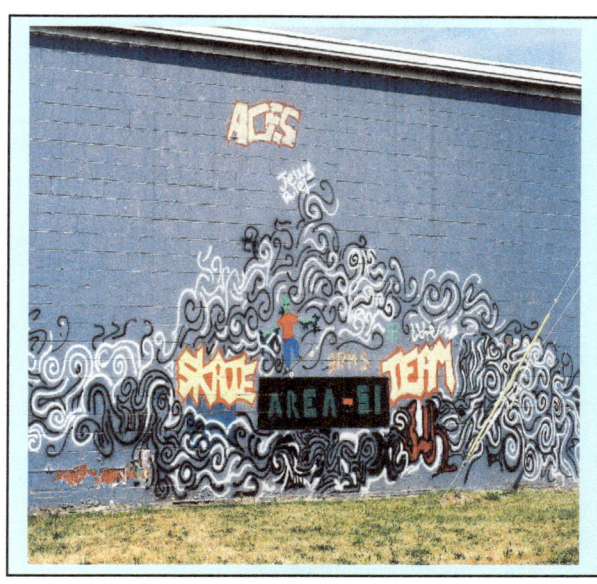

"There were hundreds and hundreds of empty paint cans on the back of the building," says ICD President Ed Arkin, who approved of early graffiti on the wall. When taggers became bold enough to deface the artists' work, the Wall of Fame quickly deteriorated into the Wall of Shame.

Some of the graffiti says: *Aces, Broad Ripple Skate Team, Jews Rule and Live your passion, Get an Education.*
"It was a war between the artists and the taggers," says Arkin, "and I had a war myself with the building against the painters." The expansion of the Monon threatened to make what had been a private wall a public spectacle and Arkin soon pulled the plug on his open-art project.

It wasn't long before a local bomber, who goes by the name of BAKS, struck back, smothering an ICD employee's car with red spray paint. [26] The graffiti here at the time of this picture (2005) recalls urban art in other cities that promoted positive neighborhood values like education. "Live Your Passion, Get and Education." This one says, "Jews Rule" and Broad Ripple High School Skate Team with a skate boarder pictured.

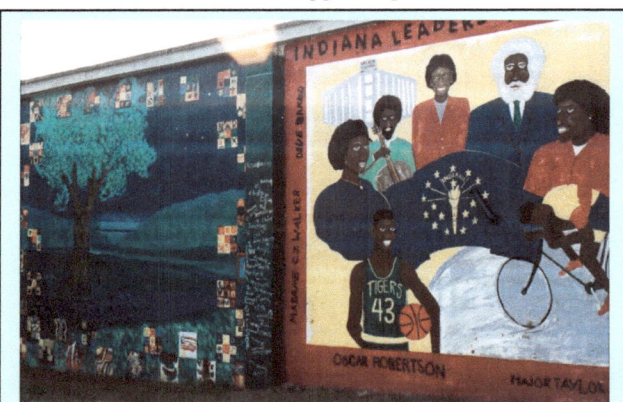

Fig. 6-27 **Indiana Black Leaders**
Just north of 49th street are more theme murals, one by the Indianapolis Hebrew Congregation on "Our World, Our Responsibility" (next page) and this one picturing Indiana Black Leaders and a nature scene.

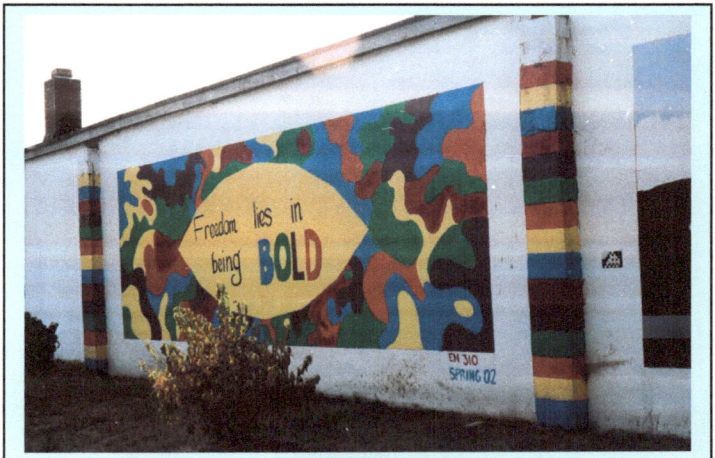

Fig. 6-28 **Freedom is in being bold.** Same location as above.

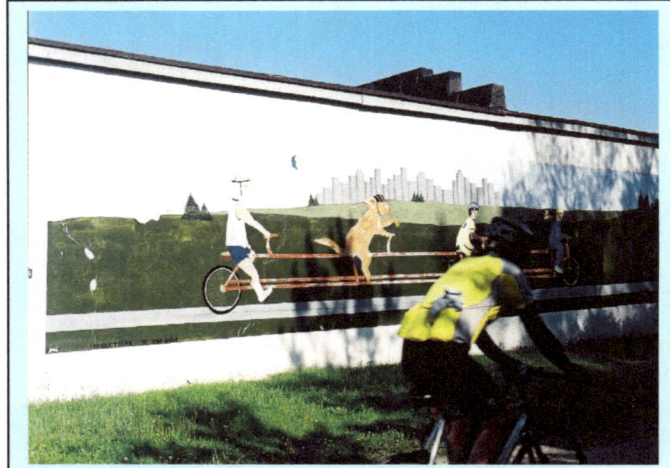

Fig. 6-29 Same location

Fig. 6-30 **Our World Our Responsibility**
Artists: Indianapolis Hebrew Congregation

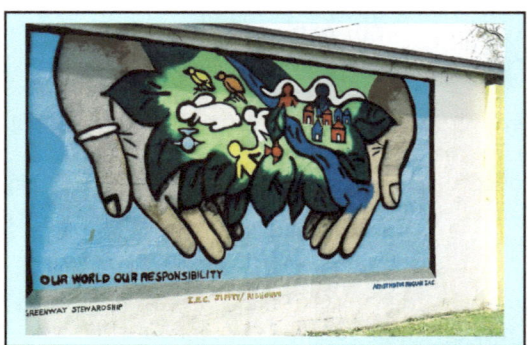

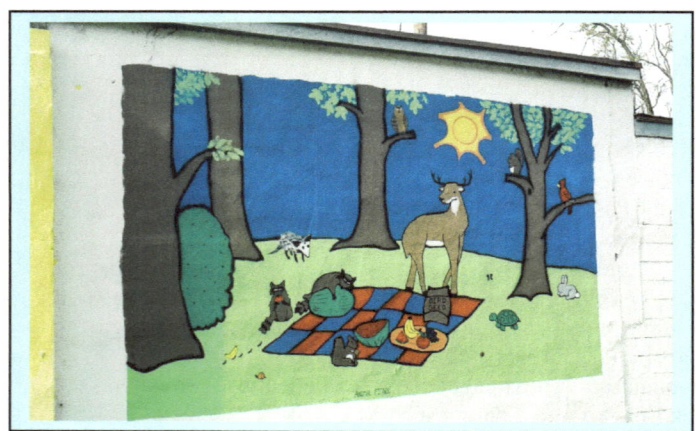

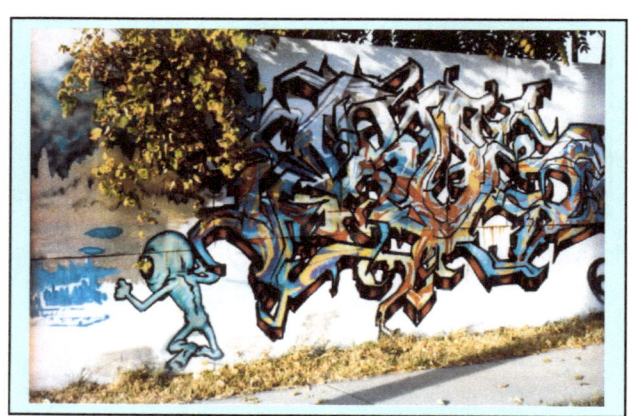

Fig 6-31 Indianapolis Hebrew Congregation

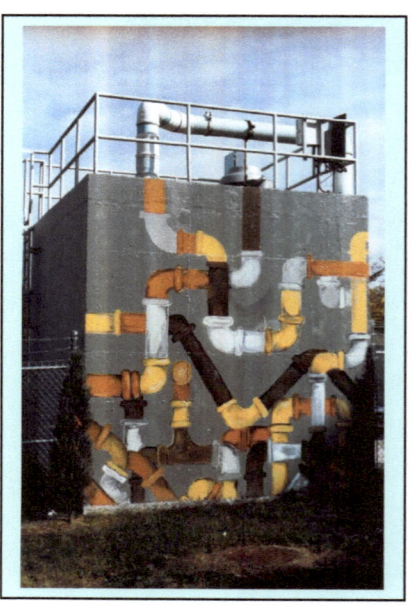

Fig 6-32 Joshua Wells FAB Fabulous Aerosol Brothers

Fig. 6-33-34 **Monon Trail** south of 38th street

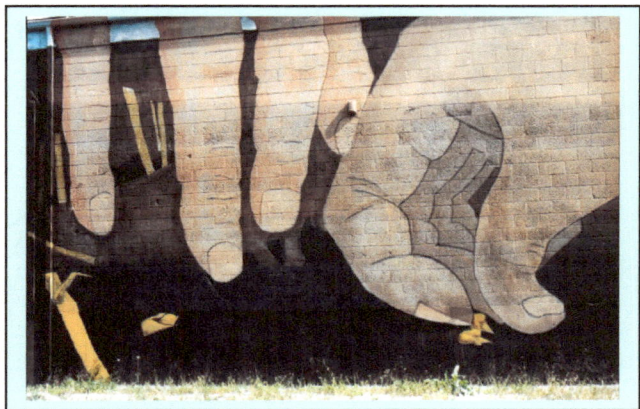

Fig. 6-35 **The Gleaners**

The block-long mural is artist Julian Gammons' interpretation of Jean-Francois Millet's 19th Century painting "The Gleaners" and is located along the Monon Trail on the west wall of Gleaners Food Bank located at 1102 E. 16th Street in Indianapolis.

The artist's own interpretation of the painting is farther north on the wall in the form of giant stalks of wheat that blend with the real grass in front of the mural. Its hard to tell where the real grass ends and the painting begins.

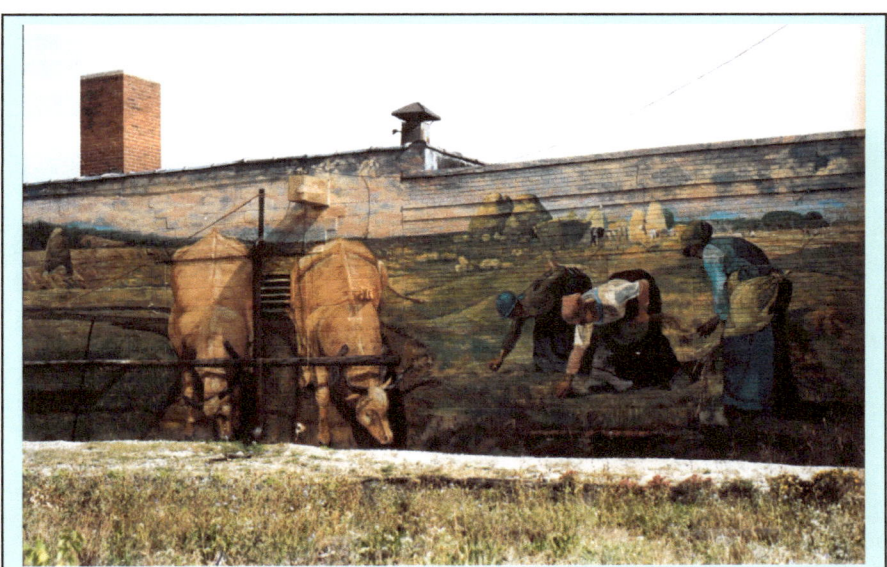

Fig. 6-36 Same

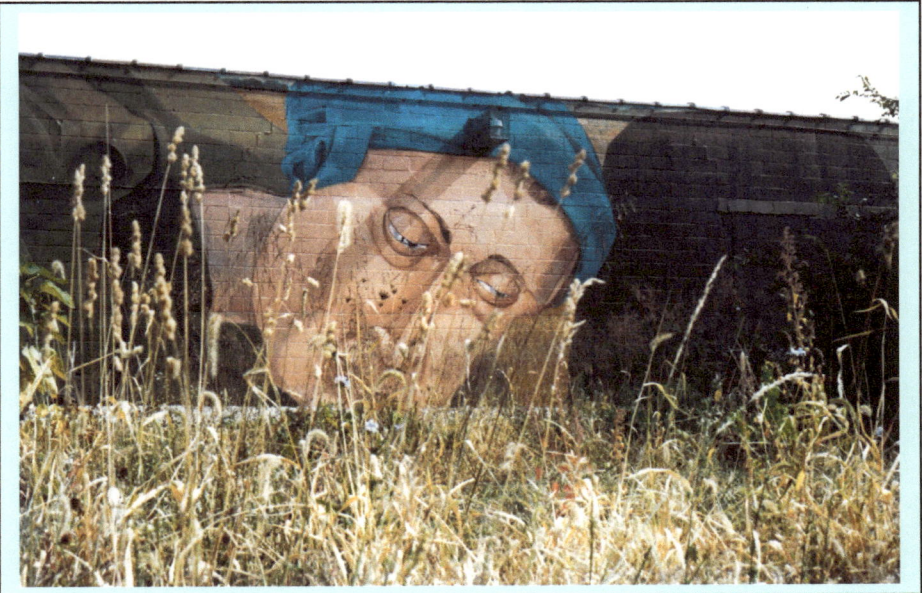

Fig. 6-37 Same

53

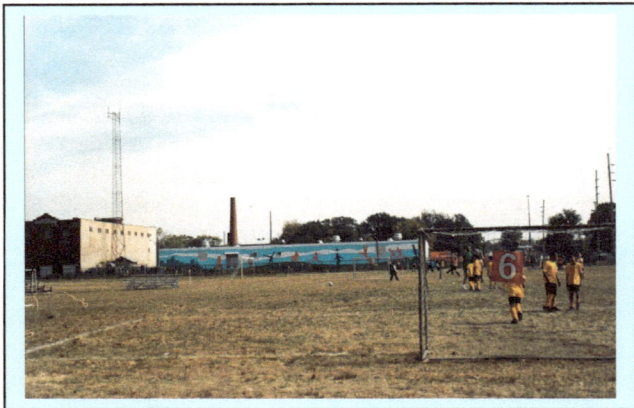

Fig. 6-38 **The Frank and Judy O'Bannon Old Northside Soccer Park Mural.**

Approximately 17 acres of land for the soccer park, located on the eastern edge of the neighborhood, was leased to the Foundation from the State of Indiana. Since 1998 it has been home to Tab Soccer, the Hispanic Center's summer youth soccer league, and the Indianapolis Christian School. The park serves as a trailhead and parking for the Monon Trail. In 2003 the park become part of the Indy Parks system. At that time the name was changed to honor and recognize the role that former ONS residents Frank and Judy O'Bannon served to create this park. Even with Indy Parks management, the ONS neighborhood has remained active in the future use and development of the park.

Across from the Frank and Judy O'Bannon Soccer Park, is a mural showing people on the trail and the skyline done by YMCA and Greenways for the National Governor's Association meeting in Indy. [38]

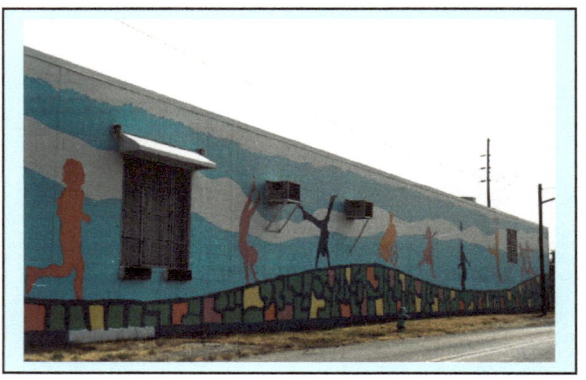

Fig. 6-39 **Same**

The mission of the Old Northside Neighborhood Association is to create a total urban community with a respect for the past. The Association strives to provide a sense of community among neighbors by blending an historic 19th Century neighborhood with a commitment to create a vibrant, modern and diverse future. [39]

Fig. 6-40 **Trail Angel** From article about National Mayors Ride 2004. (Jim's trike in front of lighted statue

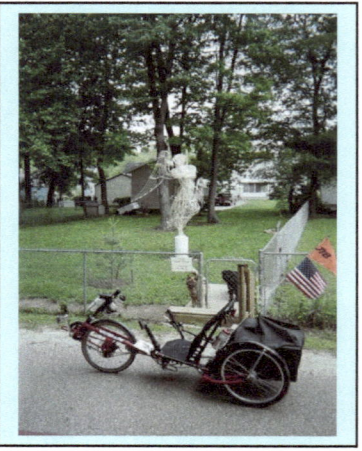

on Monan Trail that one of the trailside homes had built.)

Along the Monon trail the neighbors have become very innovative. One set up an air hose, water and a little shelter to fix people's bikes. Another has made an angel all out of vines and branches, they even light it up at night. It is about 15 feet tall, beautiful and I got a picture. We were honored to be received by Kristin Weaver, a charming young woman who is in charge of PR for their Parks and Rec. They even have a whole department for Indy Greenways. I do believe of all the cities I have been in that this is the most impressive. Mainly due to the businesses that have developed along the trails that are demonstrating what an asset biking can be to a community. May 23, 2003 National Bicycle Greenways Day Mayors' Ride from Columbus, Ohio to Indianapolis. [40]

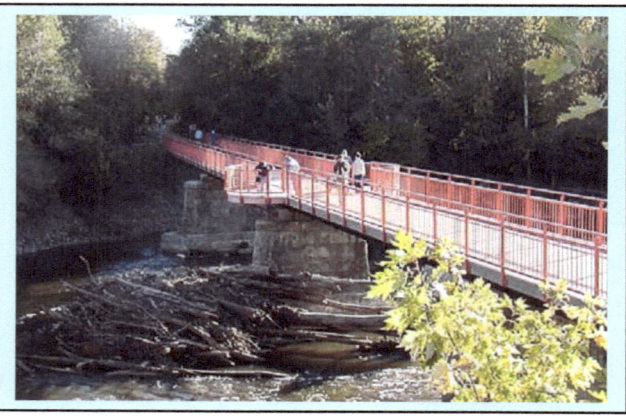

Fig. 6-41 **Monon Trail - 10 years old in 2006**

Born of grassroots citizen efforts in the mid-1980s, the Monon Trail came to life because of the creation of Indy Parks Greenways and the appointment of Ray Irvin as administrator in 1989. The first section, from Nora to Broad Ripple, opened in 1996.

Downtown connection With the completion of the South Monon, cyclists can make a simple jog to Massachusetts Avenue and downtown -- or connect to the White River Trail. UCLA researcher Antoinette Yancey was impressed with the connections between neighborhoods. The city's bike trail system has quite a few miles to go before it connects the entire county. But it may have been invented just in time to help with a health crisis that can be reversed with exercise. The Eastside has started the Pensy trail along the old Pennsylvania Railroad tracks that run parallel to Washington Street from Ritter Avenue to German Church Road and other trails are planned including the Eagle Creek Greenway on the West Side. [41]

Note: Please see Volume III of Indianapolis Murals, Outside Public Art for Chapaters on Graffiti and Aerosol Art, Styles of Painting used in the murals and the Mural Artists.

Monon Trail Photo List and Sources
1. Intro.
  [1]Ray Irvin: A Man on a Mission by Michael J. Nolan (www.indianapoliseye.com)
  Monday, December 30, 2002 and Happy trails to greenways chief, January 28, 2006 Editorial by the Star. Editorial section
2. Tuchman Cleaners 1470 E. 86th Dan Mitchell – Monon Mural
3. Arthur Jordan YMCA – Nora - Linda Lowman 2004
4. Monon trail – mosaic pillars
  [4] http://www.inasla.org/schoolfortheblind.htm
5. Whistle Stop and sculptured mural near 65th.
6. Shoes near 65th.
7. Kurz 64th St. mural.
  [7] http://www.indygreenways.org/igdc/igdc-min_nov05.htm
8. - 25. The Nature of Indy – 2004 Murals by school children celebrating nature.
26. Wall of Fame – near 52nd and College Graffiti
  [26] Nuvo article on Grafitti http://www.nuvo.net/archive/111899/111899_acover.html
      "Dropping the Bomb" by Jason Yoder
27. -31. Just north of 49th street, more theme murals and Indianapolis Hebrew Congregation Mural
32. Joshua Wells - 49th and College Trail Mural
  [32] Murals@paintsubsurface.ort
33. -34. Geometric design on Utility Building and Street Art and Graffiti and Aerosol murals around 25th St.
35. – 37. Julian Gammons – the Gleaners 16th and Monon
38 -39. Across from the Frank and Judy O,Bannon Soccer Park, is a mural showing people on the trail and the skyline done by YMCA and Greenways.
  [38- 39] http://www.oldnorthside.org/onsf.html
40. Trail Angel
  [40] http://www.bikeroute.com/NationalMayorsRide2004/#Anchor-59125
41. Trail photo – Bridge north of Art Center (66th and College)
  [41] Indianapolis Star - Monon Trail visitors like what they see, Aug 6, 2006, Russ Pulliam Editorial
42. Mural north of 49th St.

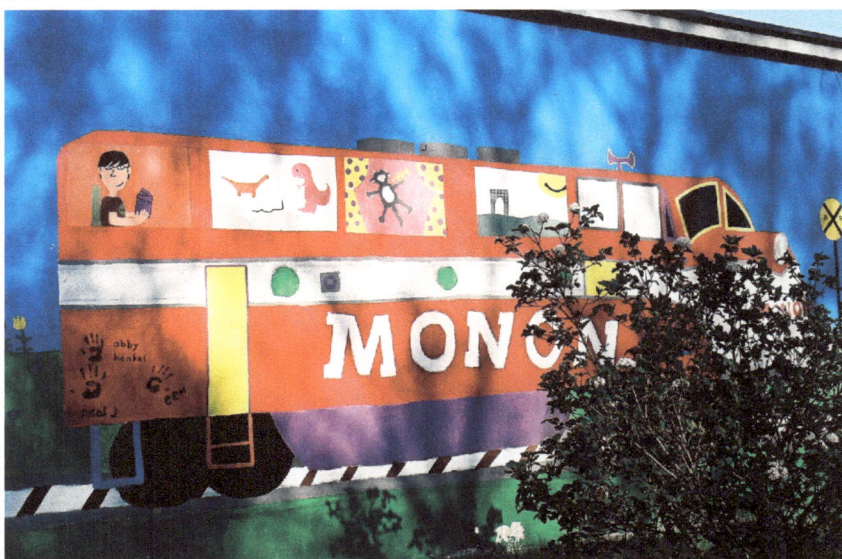

Fig. 6-42 **Monon Engine** north of 49th St.